SM99008929
5/00

D0231590

✓

056 607 8198

THE ART OF PERSUASIVE
COMMUNICATION

To Sue, Charlotte and Sam—with thanks for your unending patience, understanding and encouragement.

THE ART OF
Persuasive
COMMUNICATION

Richard Storey

Gower

Published by
Gower Publishing Limited
Gower House
Croft Road
Aldershot
Hampshire GU11 3HR
England

Gower
Old Post Road
Brookfield
Vermont 05036
USA

British Library Cataloguing in Publication Data
Storey, Richard
    The art of persuasive communication
    1. Business communication 2. Communication in management
    I. Title
    658.4'5

ISBN 0 566 07819 8

Library of Congress Cataloging-in-Publication Data
Storey, Richard, 1939–
        The art of persuasive communication / Richard Storey.
            p.   cm.
        Includes index.
        ISBN 0–566–07819–8
        1. Persuasion (Rhetoric)   I. Title
    P301.5.P47S76   1997
    808—dc21   96–40147
                                                                   CIP

Typeset in 11 on 12 pt Times by Intype London Ltd
and printed in Great Britain
at the University Press, Cambridge

Contents

Acknowledgements

Warm thanks to the many hundreds of people who have attended my training courses. They remain a constant source of energy, creative ideas and good influencing practice.

Many thanks to Carol Walker, who helped edit the manuscript, for her invaluable and constructive comments. Also to Laura Fox-Britton and Steve Rose, who checked the manuscript prior to publication. Lastly to the man who started it all by having faith in my ability to help readers influence others—my editor, Malcolm Stern.

RS

Introduction

If a man will begin with certainties, he shall end in doubts; but if he will be content to begin with doubts, he shall end in certainties. Francis Bacon

Attempts to change the opinions of others are as old as human speech, and down the years much thought and discussion has centred on the business of 'influence'. One of the earliest books on the subject, first printed in 1922, was called *Self-mastery through Conscious Autosuggestion* by Emile Coué (George Allen & Unwin). Its companion volume was Charles Baudouin's *Suggestion and Autosuggestion*. One of the world's best-selling books (well over six million at the last count), *How to Win Friends and Influence People*, was written by Dale Carnegie in 1938.

So persuasion is not a new subject. However, most people do not consider that 'influence' or 'persuasion' is a necessary part of their job. These are skills taught to salespeople and are a world away from their own lives. As a result we often prefer to think that our communications with others are designed to inform rather than persuade. Nothing could be further from the truth. Every day we all try to change the beliefs, ideas or minds of other people. Communicating

1

information will always include the aim that the receiver accepts and believes what we have told them. A doctor friend of mine freely admits that he filters the facts he wants people to hear. For example, he regularly tells patients that smoking is proved to be bad for their health. He does not tell them that his father, now in his eighties, has smoked 40 cigarettes a day all his life. Don't fool yourself—we rarely give facts to people without wanting to influence or persuade them in some way. 'Giving the facts' will often include leaving some facts out altogether. If this is the case, how about this for a definition of influencing:

> Providing the right amount of information for another person with the intent to produce a change.

The changes brought about could include a change in beliefs, attitude, thinking, feelings or behaviours. Whether we are prepared to admit it or not we are involved in the persuasion process. Nowadays the word 'persuasion' brings with it some undesirable baggage. Baggage which usually includes the idea of manipulation. Unfortunately the word 'persuasion' has acquired negative connotations. Hidden techniques of the advertising profession, military brainwashing, political propaganda have all contributed to the way that persuasion is regarded. Of course it is simple for anyone to use influencing or persuasion skills for manipulative purposes. A boxer is taught boxing skills and can apply them very effectively in the ring to great acclaim and financial reward. If those same skills are employed outside the boxing ring, then condemnation is likely to follow. Plus a fine or jail sentence.

It all depends on you. On why you want to learn influencing skills and to what uses you will put them. If our influencing is conducted fairly and honourably with a genuine desire to create benefits for others then whether we call it 'influencing', 'convincing' or 'persuasion' should not matter. We can sleep easily with our integrity intact.

At this point it seems appropriate to emphasize that *The Art of Persuasive Communication* is designed mainly as a 'do-it-yourself influencing kit'. It is not an academic text on the psychological principles involved although it contains references to the relevant research. There are several clear solutions to influencing problems and concerns but there is no recommended 'best' approach to influence. As the reader you are invited throughout to examine specific concerns of your own and to develop them with the skills, strategies, tactics and techniques outlined.

Increasingly, our success in life is measured through our ability to influence people at work and socially. No-one today can afford to be without influencing skills. A good opportunity crops up just as often in the pub, or over a meal, as it does in the workplace. With jobs at a premium and more people becoming self-employed, we all need to master the skills of influencing others in order to make the most of these opportunities. Recently, the American Management Association surveyed 2800 executives. They asked 'What is the No. 1 need for success in business today?' The overwhelming response was:

To persuade others of my value and the value of my ideas.

How often does the need to influence others enter your life? Once a month? Twice a week? The chances are that, like most people, you need to bring your influence to bear several times every day. Influencing others is certainly easier if you are in a position of authority, or have power over others. But what happens if you don't have any authority, or lack the power to control other people's actions or thoughts? Salespeople are highly skilled in influencing. Perhaps you have not had the advantage of sales training (or maybe you do not see yourself as a 'sales' type). We all know someone who possesses the 'gift of the gab' or has kissed the Blarney stone.

Most people achieve success in influencing through their natural instincts—or a good measure of luck. Without proper training or an understanding of the secrets of successful persuaders, you can easily become frustrated because you can't seem to communicate your creative ideas. You feel ignored, become discouraged and miss good opportunities. The result is that you give up altogether, or remain ignored by your boss, colleagues, friends or partner.

Don't despair. Those secrets used by successful persuaders can be easily learned and elegantly used by anyone—even those in a subordinate position. Quick and measurable success can follow; and with it, the feeling of being ignored by others becomes a thing of the past.

The Art of Persuasive Communication is for those of you who want to make their mark in a competitive environment, gain promotion, convince their boss, their family, their friends and win customers over. At work or socially you should gain in confidence and see career opportunities develop. Most importantly, perhaps for the first time, you will realize that the power to influence is not exclusively available to those in authority. With hands-on skills and a proactive attitude you, too, can take charge of your life and career.

The book is chiefly aimed at influencing one to one or within small groups (up to four people) and is designed to take you, step by step, down the path to increased success. Although you will already know and use some of the techniques and methods it teaches, there are sure to be many tips and hints which are new, or forgotten. When you add these extra tools to your communication tool kit, influencing others will not only be more rewarding—it will be fun, too.

What do you want from this book?

As we have already seen, the term 'influencing' means different things to different people. It often depends on who you are influencing and the way you intend to go about it. The dictionary defines influencing as: 'the power of producing an effect, bringing something about, especially unobtrusively'. This can embrace persuasion, convincing, negotiating and even selling. The key word is 'unobtrusively'. Influencing may mean simply 'having your own way'. It is for you, the reader, to decide what kind of influencing you usually carry out. This will probably depend on where (at home, socially or at work), when (spontaneously or with plenty of notice and forward planning) and how (face to face, on the telephone, at a meeting, in a presentation, in writing).

Which of these areas of influence is of particular concern to you, and what are your typical objectives? Ask yourself which of these suits your personal style:

- helping others to reach the right conclusion, with integrity
- having some influence over an outcome
- persuading others to do something you want them to do
- convincing people that your suggestions are of benefit
- selling your ideas and proposals to others
- making people change their minds, or arrive at some conclusion
- obtaining agreement to change
- extracting a decision from someone
- making convincing presentations
- managing a project
- influencing senior groups
- convincing internal customers
- influencing outcomes
- improving an image
- gaining acceptance
- negotiating successfully
- gaining compliance
- selling something
- changing perceptions
- altering attitudes
- managing performance
- changing beliefs
- change design
- improving supplier performance
- managing a process
- managing relationships
- improving social influence
- gaining initial entry to prospective customers/clients
- having new ideas accepted by experienced people
- influencing groups or meetings
- writing convincing proposals

- changing divergence into convergence
- influencing others on the telephone.

Know thyself

If you were to describe yourself as an influencer, what words would you use? Be honest—self-appraisal is the first step towards personal improvement (or be brave and ask someone who knows you well to complete this section for you).

What are your greatest strengths as an influencer?

What weaknesses do you have as an influencer?

What would you like people to say about your influencing skills?

What sort of influencer do you want to become?

- Show this self-analysis to a friend or colleague— someone who knows your influencing style and approach. Do they see you in the same way?
- When you next influence people, use and develop further your greatest strength.
- Start an action plan now to reduce or eliminate your weaknesses.

What skills do you need to develop?

The following are the most common aims people have when they intend to influence another person, or people. Use the boxes to rate how confident you are of achieving your aims (each area is covered by a separate chapter):

Ratings
5 I am completely confident
4 I am very confident
3 I am confident
2 I am reasonably confident
1 I am not at all confident

Thinking of a forthcoming influencing situation:

❑ I want to clarify my objectives (Chapter 1)
❑ I want to find out what inner values and beliefs drive the other person (Chapter 2)
❑ I want to establish the needs of others (Chapter 3)
❑ I want to show how my proposals will be of benefit to them (Chapter 4)
❑ I want to be able to have greater rapport with a wider variety of people (Chapter 5)
❑ I want to improve my understanding of non-verbal communication (Chapter 6)
❑ I want to be able to deal with different personalities (Chapter 7)
❑ I want the flexibility to use a variety of influencing styles (Chapter 8)
❑ I want to be able to overcome any objections to my proposals (Chapter 9)
❑ I want to ensure that decisions are made—and in my favour (Chapter 10)
❑ I want to improve my influence at meetings and presentations (Chapter 11)
❑ I want to convince people on the telephone (Chapter 12)
❑ I want to improve my ability to influence in reports, proposals and letters (Chapter 13)

Now—add up your total score:

13	26	39	52	65
Not at all confident	Reasonably confident	Confident	Very confident	Completely confident

Which of these aims did you mark with a 1 or a 2? If you don't have the time to read the whole of this book now, read only those chapters that are of immediate concern to you.

Using the exercises

Each chapter contains one or more exercises. When the chapter content covers a particular aim of yours, read through the exercises and select one or more to follow. Complete the exercise (or modify it to suit) and notice the results it brings. Use these to help develop strengths and eradicate weaknesses.

Develop a personal exercise

You may decide that it will be more useful to create your own exercise. On influencing skills training courses that I run we encourage participants to think of a real influencing situation that they will have to face when the course ends. As the course progresses, participants map their new knowledge directly on to their forthcoming influencing situation.

The response we receive to this approach is very positive and rewarding. Countless course attendees have telephoned, written or faxed to tell me about their successes. For some, this approach can be of more direct use than always working through the specific exercises in each chapter.

Choosing the right path

There are many approaches to influence. Several of these are outlined in Chapter 8. Experiment with an approach which is unusual for you. See where and how it works, making changes to suit your own style. In the appendix at the end of the book you will find three 'models'. These are the classic, well-known paths to influence. They offer you further choices and can be used, in pick 'n mix fashion, to handle the different situations in which you will find yourself.

The value of role play

Do consider rehearsing your planned influencing situation with a colleague or friend. Most people understandably detest the thought of role playing. We've all been on courses where we have to role play an atypical scene in front of a room full of highly critical people—camera, lights, action and so on. What I am suggesting is altogether different. If you can find someone who knows and understands the background to your role play, get together for a while and run through your planned approach. Tell your role player what objections you are likely to receive, giving yourself the opportunity to try out some responses. Notice what works, or is less successful. Be aware of your state—how do you feel during certain parts of your role play? Use the information gained to adjust your final influencing approach.

Role play is especially important if you are planning to influence a group. Encourage friends or colleagues to throw questions at you or challenge your conclusions and recommendations. I can guarantee that, after developing and running a well-thought-out role play, as they say in the theatre 'on the night' you should experience a wonderfully satisfying feeling of *déjà vu* as well as a sense of confidence that comes with experience.

And finally . . .

The communication tools which this book contains will help you to think about how you approach others and will help you perform with greater accuracy and success. By implementing the suggested sequences and developing greater flexibility in your approach many communication problems will simply disappear. You will achieve more objectives, communicate better with a wider range of people and—above all—become known as a successful influencer.

Chapter 1

Setting personal objectives

All men dream: but not equally. Those who dream by night in the dusty recesses of their minds wake in the day to find it was vanity: but the dreamers of the day are dangerous men, for they may act their dreams with open eyes, to make it possible. T.E. Lawrence

This chapter examines the need for planning to influence, the value of setting well-formed influencing objectives and the dividends to be gained from role play practice.

For many people the subject of objective setting has become a bore. We have all read about the need for objectives, seen the training video and attended the course. Setting objectives for ourselves is seldom easy and the process itself can be tedious. It is a discipline which most of us acknowledge—then choose to ignore. Objective setting is rather like time management: you have the highest hopes and aspirations, but often nothing really changes because the actual business of setting an objective does not in itself change anything. For an objective to be achieved we have to work at it. It means effort, commitment and self-discipline. So why start this book with a whole chapter devoted to the subject?

In the 1950s Yale University produced a detailed study of how and why certain students became more successful than others after graduating. The study included the gender, race, height and hair colouring of students. It also looked at goal setting. Students were asked what their future objectives were and how they went about setting them. Only 3% of the sample group had written down their life goals. Twenty years later, when a follow-up study was carried out, the 3% who had identified and put objectives in writing were more successful and worth more in financial terms than the other 97% put together.

Two good reasons for setting influencing objectives

- Objective setting is arguably the single most important aspect of the influencing process. It is the first step you take. After focusing on where you want to go and examining how your objectives might overlap those of the person or people who you want to influence you will find that most of the remaining steps fall into place.
- Setting clearly defined objectives and writing them down actually works.

If you think objective setting is outdated or if you lack the personal discipline needed, you will find it of practical value to re-think your attitude to objectives and goals.

How we programme our brain to achieve unconscious objectives

You may or may not be consciously aware that you already set objectives for yourself. As you live your days, weeks and years you are constantly moving towards objective achievement. Take a simple procedure—getting up in the morning to go to work. There are things you do automatically. You brush your teeth, shower, get dressed, eat breakfast, leave the house. There may be other things that you could do: repaint the front door, read a novel, clean the bathroom, telephone your aunt in Australia. But you don't. These tasks may be on your 'to do list' but you put them to one side because you know unconsciously that they would prevent you from reaching your objective of getting to work. You have objectives all the time, if only to do nothing but relax. With no *conscious* objectives you would be aimless and achieve very little.

Within larger objectives, such as getting to work, are smaller ones. For instance, when you dress you may wish to look smart, so you check that your clothing is clean—almost without realizing it. This is because you've set your objective and find yourself automatically moving towards it without considering each small step along the way. Our conscious minds can handle up to nine separate pieces of information at any one time. As we get out of bed, we're already thinking about our bathroom routine, mentally running through our first meeting at the same time as we listen to the radio and peer out of the window to examine today's weather. Yet during these complex thought processes our bodies perform micro-muscle movements and demanding mechanical feats without consciously being asked to. If we had to think about several thousand things at once, our conscious minds simply couldn't cope. So we select what to pay attention to. We sort what to do, what to ignore, to what we should give our time and energy. Our criteria for whether actions or thoughts are useful to us are generated by knowing our aims. Our brains are programmed and we achieve our unconscious objectives without much thought or effort.

There are two types of basic influencing situations. The first is where you have some idea of what is about to happen and the role you are to play in influencing the outcome— the conscious objective. The other is where you have little or no advance warning that you are going to have to influence anything or anyone—the unconscious objective. This extract, taken from a news item in *The Times*, shows clearly how, with no prior warning, the need to influence can become a downright necessity. The programmed brain somehow swings into action and achieves the objective for us.

A couple of years ago my eye was caught by a headline. It read: 'Pensioner Talks Thieves into Giving Back Money.' I read on. Apparently an old lady, aged 80, was sitting alone at home one evening when three masked men broke into her house. She was naturally terrified. She obviously had several choices but, perhaps surprisingly, chose the least likely—submissive persuasion. One burglar tied her to the chair while the others ransacked the house finding some money and a few pieces of silver. She explained to the men that she knew why they were doing this—they were poor, like her, had no money and nothing to look forward to in life. She went on: 'I am so cold in the winter that I have to sit with a hot water bottle on my knees as I can't afford to heat the house.'

Eventually, she showed so much empathy (and sympathy) that one of the burglars said 'Here, you can have this back' and handed her the money and her valuables. They left her, still tied up, without taking a penny.

Afterwards, she said: 'The police told me they had never heard anything like it.'

Life is punctuated with incidents and moments when you will need to influence people and circumstances. Some may be dangerous, as in the case of that old lady, others less tricky. Even so, with no warning, most of us have to rely on our instincts and gut reactions. After a while many repeat influencing situations will be dealt with automatically, efficiently, effectively and unconsciously. Your subconscious will register prior success and will guide you towards a predictable outcome. When this takes place you will begin to develop a reputation as a confident and successful influencer. Even if you are caught unawares your pre-programmed brain will take over and steer you towards a satisfactory conclusion. But be warned. It is here that the trouble really starts. Perhaps you may have become complacent and overconfident. Influencing others becomes a matter of course or of habit.

Why it is important to understand what influences you

When you become fully aware of *how* the influence process works you will be able to use tools and techniques with more precision—and come to depend on a more reliable and predictable outcome. A useful way to begin to understand this business of setting specific influencing objectives is to analyse what it is that influences *you*.

Think back to a time when you were influenced by another person. Recall the steps or elements of their influence. What did they do or say that convinced you? What were the key words and phrases? Where did the conversation take place? What was their manner like? What was your own frame of mind, or mood? If you used the same approach with others, could you be sure that it would be effective? Chances are that you would need to make modifications to your approach, changes which would take into account:

- your frame of mind
- the other person's mood
- their age
- their gender
- their cultural background
- their relationship to you
- their understanding or experience of the subject
- the time of day, week or year
- the location of the meeting
- their ability or desire to listen
- their interpretative skills
- their willingness to be influenced by you
- the way in which they like to make decisions.

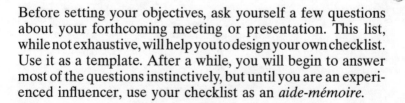

Before setting your objectives, ask yourself a few questions about your forthcoming meeting or presentation. This list, while not exhaustive, will help you to design your own checklist. Use it as a template. After a while, you will begin to answer most of the questions instinctively, but until you are an experienced influencer, use your checklist as an *aide-mémoire*.

Influencing checklist

Person, people, meeting participants, group or audience to be influenced:

Your objectives? What do you want to happen as a result of your successful influence?

Their objectives—what do they want to happen?

What gap if any exists between your objectives and their objectives?

Continued

Analysis of the other person or people involved:

A. Their knowledge of the subject:

❑   High level   ❑   General   ❑   Limited
❑   None   ❑   Unknown

B. Their likely opinions about you/your motives/the subject/your organization:

❑   **Very favourable**   ❑   **Favourable**   ❑   **Neutral**
❑   **Slightly hostile**   ❑   **Very hostile**   ❑   **Unknown**

C. Their reasons or motives for attending:

D. Disadvantages and advantages of your objectives to them as individuals, or as a group:

Advantages

Disadvantages

Continued

E. General analysis (work related):

What are their occupational relationships to you, your department or organization?
- ❏ Existing customer
- ❏ New customer
- ❏ Top management
- ❏ Middle management
- ❏ People you manage
- ❏ Other management
- ❏ Other colleagues
- ❏ The public
- ❏ Outside agencies

Their familiarity with your company's business activities?
- ❏ Very familiar
- ❏ Moderately familiar
- ❏ Unfamiliar

Their understanding of your technical vocabulary?
- ❏ Technical
- ❏ Non-technical
- ❏ Generally high
- ❏ Low
- ❏ Unknown

Open-mindedness—willingness to accept new ideas?
- ❏ Eager
- ❏ Open
- ❏ Neutral
- ❏ Slightly resistant
- ❏ Strongly resistant
- ❏ Unknown

Information most likely to gain their attention and influence this audience?
- ❏ Highly technical information
- ❏ Statistical comparisons
- ❏ Pictures
- ❏ Cost figures
- ❏ Metaphor
- ❏ Demonstrations
- ❏ Lecture style
- ❏ Questions
- ❏ Dialogue
- ❏ Anecdotal evidence
- ❏ Unknown

> *Continued*
>
> **Techniques/information likely to provoke negative
> attitudes/response?**
>
>
> **Summarize, in a few sentences/phrases, the most
> important information gained from the preceding
> sections.**

Clarifying your conscious objectives

Before you commence your plan to influence, think clearly
about your objectives. What do you want to happen as
a result of influencing this person/people? Here are some
questions which you may want to ask yourself even before
you start to formulate your objective statement. Use the
above checklist and be sure that you have the answers to
the following questions:

- Why do I want to influence this person?
- What will I gain when I succeed in doing so?
- What are his/her objectives?
- How do his/her objectives dovetail with my own?
- What will he/she gain from my influence?
- Are there any ethical or moral concerns which I need
  to consider?
- Will my success in influencing be of mutual benefit?
- When I have succeeded, will my integrity remain
  intact?
- Will any other people be adversely affected by the
  outcome?

- Will my success in any way alter future attempts to influence this person?

Integrity, ethics and morals

There are of course no practical reasons why considerations of ethics, morals or integrity need ever enter the argument. That is for you to decide. Before you start, ask yourself two questions. Will I ever have to influence this person again? To what extent am I concerned that I preserve my ongoing relationship with this person?

Professionals who sell or negotiate for a living will continually ask these questions of themselves. Take two influencers. The first wants to sell you their house. They are most unlikely to need to sell you a house ever again so could, if they chose, use pressure, exaggeration or outright lying to achieve their aim. The second influencer is a professional financial adviser. They advise on matters concerning life assurance and pension plans. They have a very strong need to retain their client's trust and to sustain and develop a continuing business relationship. In their case, it would be counter-productive to oversell or make untrue claims about their products.

How to set your conscious objectives

The 80-year-old pensioner who persuaded the burglars to return her money had no time to set any influencing objectives, let alone write them down. She immediately realized that her possessions and possibly her life were under threat—and just got on with the business of persuading. Suppose you are due to have an important meeting with a friend or a colleague, where you will be required to state your case and convince others. You have time to work out your strategy, to consider how you will handle objections to your proposal and so on. You also have time to set personal objectives. At the beginning of this chapter we acknowledged that we often talk about the importance of objective setting; we pay lip service to it but rarely do more than say something like:

> I really want to win them over.
> I know I'm right and I'm going to try to sell them on the idea.
> I don't want this to go on any longer and I am going to do my best to convince them to stop doing it.
> I hope to persuade them that they are making the wrong decision.

These are not objectives—they are hopes, aspirations, wish lists. 'Nothing wrong with that,' some might say. 'At least I have an idea of what I want to achieve.' There is no harm in having a rough idea of what you want to do. Nor is it wrong to set out to achieve something specific, attainable and lasting. But there is a world of difference between the two approaches.

Stop for a moment and analyse the four 'objectives' listed above.

1. *I really want to win them over.*

Full marks for determination. But determination alone will not necessarily mean that your objectives 'to win them over' are met.

2. *I know I'm right and I am going to try to sell them on the idea.*

The very inclusion of the verb 'to try' acknowledges the possibility of failure.

3. *I don't want this to go on any longer and I am going to do my best to convince them to stop doing it.*

This is a negative objective. You are attempting to convince people *not* to do something.

4. *I hope to persuade them that they are making the wrong decision.*

The aspiration 'I hope' is rather like 'to try', suggesting the likelihood of only partial success or even downright failure.

The five-step approach to objective setting

Setting objectives is the core of professional success. Unfortunately it is not simply a matter of announcing to yourself (or more publicly) 'I am going to achieve such and such'. Certainly, this is a beginning—but it is only the beginning. Several other factors need examining if your dream is to come true. When you next set an objective or make a goal, follow this five-step approach and as you do so notice two things: first, how this systematic approach forces you to examine your objectives and, secondly, how you suddenly become a person who actually achieves their objectives.

Step one—think positively

Make certain that your objective is stated in *the positive*; think of what you *want* as well as what you don't want.

> **Example:** 'I don't want this to go on any longer.'
> **Q.**   'What would you prefer to happen?'
> **A.**   'I want things to go right in future.'

'I don't want this to go on any longer' gives you no specific aim.

Step two—put yourself in charge

Think of the part you will play in achieving the outcome. Make certain that the possibility of achievement is within your control, not someone else's.

> **Q.**   'What will I be doing to achieve my objective?' or 'What is my part in this?'
> **A.**   'I want to make certain that I am the one who sets the agenda for the meeting'

rather than 'I will accept the agenda and hope there will be a moment when I can explain my point of view', which is out of your complete control.

Step three—be very specific about the ways in which you will ensure your objective is met

State your objective in manageable proportions that also make it seem real; something definite to go for, which begins to suggest genuine actions towards the outcome.

Q. 'Who will I meet? What will I say? When will I talk to them? How will I approach it? Which method will I choose? Where will this take place?'

A. 'I will meet the subcommittee at their next meeting and make a presentation to them at the end of the meeting. I will raise some questions and ask them what they want. Finally, I will ask for a decision and an action plan'

rather than 'I want the Club to be more successful'—the statement is too vague.

Step four—what evidence will prove to you that you have achieved your objective?

Obtain evidence criteria. This is the sensory information which lets you know when you have achieved your goals. This will make your objective far more real and compelling.
   Use all your senses:

- sight—the evidence you will see;
- sound—the evidence you will hear;
- feeling (1)—the evidence you will sense emotionally;
- feeling (2)—the evidence you will touch;
- smell—the evidence you will smell;
- taste—the evidence you will taste.

Recently, I was helping a friend to set some influencing objectives. She wanted to persuade her husband to join her on a much needed holiday in Greece. When it came to deciding what evidence would prove to Gill that she had achieved her objective I asked her:

Q. 'What will you see, hear and feel both inside and outside that will let you know that you have achieved your objective?'

A. 'I will *see* the blue sky above me and *hear* the sound of waves, Greek music wafting through the olive grove and the clink of ice in the glass in my hand. I will *feel* the sun on my body and the cold glass in my hand. I will *smell* sun oil and the ouzo in the glass.'

Her answer was more substantial and robust than 'I'll just know when I am successful', which usually means just the opposite. You probably have no idea of your own 'buying signals' yet.

Step five—check the integrity and acceptability of your objective

Check that only consequences that you really want will result. Will you be entirely happy with the outcome? Notice any doubts, which usually start 'Yes, but . . .'

Q. 'Does any part of me object in any way to achieving my objective?' or 'If I could achieve my objective, would I take it without reservation?'

If the answer were to be a doubtful 'Yes, but . . .' or 'Well, I'm not sure' 'As long as it didn't affect such and such . . .' and so on, there are obviously other considerations or conditions which must be woven into the objective specification. These will enable it to become an acceptable one to achieve with purely positive consequences. The 'acceptability' area is where most problems occur; people think they should attempt to achieve an objective, but deep down are worried about some spin-off consequences. If you are not fully committed at this stage, you are unlikely to achieve your objective.

Influencing objectives—the five-step path

1. Write down your objective statement. Check to make sure it is stated positively.
2. Make sure you have full control over the outcome.
3. Be specific about the ways you will go about achieving your objective.
4. Ask yourself: what evidence will I see, hear, feel, smell or taste which will confirm that I have achieved my objective?
5. Check the integrity and acceptability of your objective.

Exercise—The art of creative visualization

1. Think of a future situation where you want to influence a person or people. Decide on your objective making certain that it is well formed and positively stated. Write it down.
2. What part will you play in its achievement? Who else is involved? How might their involvement affect the outcome?
3. Choose a quiet moment and place where you will not be disturbed. Sit silently for a while and allow your whole body to relax and your mind to drift. As you sit there enjoying the luxury of this time on your own, project yourself forward to the moment when you achieve your aim.
4. Imagine that you have achieved your objective in full. Project yourself right into the scene as it might appear when you succeed. As you begin to imagine this moment in the future, create a bright, sharp focused image in your mind and stay there for a while enjoying the sensations which will accompany your future success.

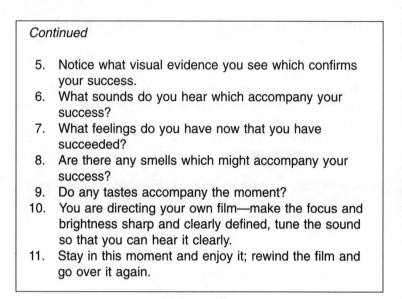

Continued

5. Notice what visual evidence you see which confirms your success.
6. What sounds do you hear which accompany your success?
7. What feelings do you have now that you have succeeded?
8. Are there any smells which might accompany your success?
9. Do any tastes accompany the moment?
10. You are directing your own film—make the focus and brightness sharp and clearly defined, tune the sound so that you can hear it clearly.
11. Stay in this moment and enjoy it; rewind the film and go over it again.

You have now set yourself up for success. Your mind and body think that your objectives have already been achieved. You will start to act and talk differently, more positively. Of course some readers may think that all of this is nonsense—until they do it for themselves and discover that it really does work. Once you make this work for yourself, creative visualization will become an everyday part of your continuing success.

The art of visualizing a future outcome is arguably the single most powerful self-development tool which you can use when influencing others or aiming for any other objective. Do not fall into the trap of limiting your success by setting yourself rigid process elements. These might include phrases such as 'By the end of the meeting I will have convinced . . .' or 'The committee members will resolve . . .' You may run the risk of painting yourself into a corner and may consider that you have 'failed' before you have had the opportunity of exploring all the options available to you.

Behaving 'as if' you will succeed

A good deal of your success as an influencer will depend on your ability to act 'as if' you are going to be successful. This does not mean looking or sounding overconfident or behaving in an arrogant manner. Behaving 'as if' simply means that your whole being is tuned towards a successful outcome. You have already visualized your objective and programmed your brain towards eventual success. Now it is the turn of your posture, speech and gesture.

Imagine this scenario. Last week you bought an expensive item from a high street store. When you made the purchase you noticed that there was a large sign saying: 'No cash refunds can be given for any items bought here'. But the friend who you bought the present for already has one so you decide to try your hand at influencing the store manager—you want a full cash refund. The conversation might go something like this:

> Er, could I have a quick word with the manager, please? Oh, you are the manageress. Right. Um, I bought this item in your shop last week and I realize that you—er—have a policy of no refunds but I wondered if it would be at all possible for you to see your way clear to give me a refund on this occasion? I'd be really grateful if you could just—er—stretch a point? No? Well, I thought I'd just give it a try—you never know your luck.

This dialogue is peppered with what I call negative nasties (they are also known as 'weak modifiers' or 'conditional statements'). Whatever you call them they are death to effective and efficient influence. Each word erodes the power and clarity of your influence. There are two levels of communication, conscious and unconscious. Often we say one thing and beam out another. Other people will quickly realize that you secretly believe that you are not likely to succeed—and they will do everything in their power to help your prediction come true!

Exercise—Detecting negative nasties

The dialogue in the shop is an exaggerated example
perhaps but full of verbal signals that you are acting 'as if'
you do not expect to succeed in your quest for a refund.
How many signals does the approach contain? I put in ten—
you may detect more.

Every one of the negative nasties contains a suggestion that
you *assumed at the outset that you would not be successful.*
And you were right, weren't you? Be direct and positive,
making sure that your request is as clear as possible. Avoid
using conditional or negative words and phrases, such as:

I don't suppose . . .	*It wouldn't be possible . . .*
Hopefully . . .	*See your way clear to . . .*
Perhaps . . .	*Sorry to bother you, but . . .*
I wonder if . . .	*I realize that you don't normally . . .*
Try to . . .	*I don't know whether you could just . . .*
Just this once?	*I thought I would just try*

State your case as a question: 'Will you organize a full cash
refund, please?' 'What would have to happen for me to
receive a full cash refund?' It will be easier for the other
person to say 'yes' or provide a solution to the problem
than to refuse.

The value of rehearsal

Part of the planning process should include some sort of
rehearsal or run-through of the projected situation. This can
take one of three forms:

1.   Simply going over your approach in your head.
2.   Talking it through with a friend or colleague.

3. A full-blown practice session preferably recorded on video or audio tape for later evaluation.

Most people detest role play and this is understandable. But the value of practice cannot be stressed too highly. I once had to conduct a negotiation with two other people. As my wife and I drove to the meeting we started to run through the forthcoming dialogue. We asked ourselves questions: 'What do we want from the negotiation? What is the most we could achieve? What is the least we would be prepared to accept? What are we likely to achieve?' 'Suppose they say such and such—how will we respond?' 'If we responded in that way would they agree with what we said? If not, what could we suggest as an alternative?' 'What variables can we trade, what is their value?' And so on.

Although it was intended that I would conduct the negotiation, in the end my wife felt so confident after the brief run-through in the car that she carried it out. With a few minor exceptions we came away with exactly what we wanted—plus one or two surprising extras.

Role play is rather like a sparring match. The boxer preparing for next Saturday's big fight will engage the services of a sparring partner. It is not the intention of either man to knock out the other or to inflict serious damage. The value of the sparring match is that it allows the champion-to-be to try things out, to see how he will react on the big night.

If you can, use either video or audio recordings to provide the basis of self-analysis. It can be quite a shock seeing or hearing yourself for the first time on tape. But once this reaction is over the value which you can derive from seeing or hearing yourself is very powerful and useful. You will notice the times when you felt and acted most confidently. You will observe the weaknesses in your approach, style or argument. You will make changes and improve your strategy. You will be more confident of your abilities and will look forward to a successful dialogue or meeting.

Summary

1. Before setting your objectives run through the influencing checklist as a preliminary guide.
2. Setting influencing objectives is not only important—it works.
3. Use the five-step approach to objective setting.
4. Use creative visualization to help you achieve your goals.
5. Use role play sessions to help you discover your strengths and weaknesses.
6. Behave 'as if' you will succeed.
7. Repeated success will build on itself. The more successful you become, the more successful you become.

Chapter 2

Understanding human motivation

To sell John Brown what John Brown buys, you have to see through John Brown's eyes.

We are all motivated in different ways and by different and changing elements in our lives. This chapter emphasizes the importance of understanding what drives other people—their values and beliefs, their needs and wants.

There is an old joke which neatly sums up motivation. The entire sales force of Perky Cat Food Company was gathered for the annual sales convention. Two thousand salespeople were listening intently to the Marketing Director who was waving his arms about on the podium, giving a most enthusiastic performance.

Who's got the greatest cat food in the world?
We have! chorused the sales force.
And who's got the best advertising campaign?
We have!! came the response.
Who has the most attractive packaging?
We have!!! they shouted in glee.
Who has the best distribution network?
WE HAVE! they roared.

OK. So why aren't we selling more of our product?
The reply came loud and clear from a lone voice at the
back of the hall:
Because the damned cats don't like it.

We are all driven by motivation. Motivation to do something, not to do something, to consider the possibilities of
doing something. Imagine the scene. You are walking down
the street when a passer-by stops you. 'Can I have a word?
Good. I have the most incredible bargain to offer you. It's
a Jaguar sports coupé in silver, only 18 months old with less
than 12 000 miles on the clock. It cost over £50 000 but to
you I can let it go for £25 000—that's half-price. How about
it; what do you think?'

Well, what would you think? You may produce a cheque
book and snap up what is evidently a real bargain. You may
disbelieve the person—who are they? Do they really own
the car? You may have suspicions about the car—is it road-
worthy? Has it been stolen, or been in a crash? And the
price. Did it really cost £50 000 18 months ago? Is it worth
£25 000 now?

Worse still—you may not be motivated to buy such a car.
Suppose you can't drive? Your family is too large for a
coupé. You can't stand the colour. You detest Jaguar cars.
You are happy with your present vehicle. You can't afford
£25 000. Perhaps you normally pay even more than that for
a car.

Unless you have power over people it is difficult to influence anybody who does not have the motivation.
Advertising people will tell you that in order to bring about
change there are only three motivators:

1. need
2. greed
3. fear.

This assumption may be accurate but it is also over-simpli-
fied. Many of our decisions are governed by *a combination*
of these motivators. Take as an example life assurance. The
primary motivator is fear—but a with-profits policy which

offers the facility to borrow against it will appeal to our need (or greed).

Convincing people that they have a need is quite easy and straightforward. But convincing them to change as a result of this knowledge is difficult. Why? Because people resist change. They may accept that needs exist but other things prevent them making the change:

- lack of funds;
- lack of time;
- loyalty to current system/idea/person/product/supplier/contract;
- sheer complacency;
- fear of making the wrong decision.

Thus, although recognition of need is very powerful, change may only be brought about when it is accompanied by greed or fear (or both). I have a need to change my car. It is old, has high mileage and is becoming increasingly unreliable. But I don't have the money. I could be persuaded to borrow the money through a finance scheme, but normally pay cash. What might change my mind? Perhaps there is another car which interests me but there is only one left in the showroom (fear); the deal which is being offered expires on Saturday (greed); the new car is a 'special edition' and appeals to my vanity (additional need).

What is motivation?

Motivation is what makes us act or behave in the way we do. If we want to influence others to change we ask: 'How can I motivate them? What are their needs?'

There are two famous classifications of needs, one formulated by Abraham Maslow, the other by Frederick Herzberg. Maslow suggests that humans have a simple hierarchy of needs; one need has to be satisfied before the next one emerges.

Herzberg's research suggests that motivators at work fall into two categories. The first group spring from the work itself and include job satisfaction, recognition, a sense of achievement, good communication, belonging, social accept-ance: all real motivators. They appear to be continuous and genuinely spur us on to even better performance and effort.

The second group of needs (Herzberg's so-called 'hygiene factors' extrinsically provided by the employer) appear to be motivators but in fact are not and can even be 'de-motivators'. These include the environment, pay, holidays, training—all designed to *prevent* job dissatisfaction. For example, a pay rise is very satisfying and a good motivator, but only in the short term. Almost as soon as we bank our new salary our pay increase starts to decrease in value both in real terms and in how pleased we feel about it.

Motivation is a forward-looking process and starts with those needs and wants which exist in us all.

- Needs create action.
- Action achieves goals.
- Achieving a goal satisfies a need.

This process closely follows the path we tread when influencing:

1. identify the other person's needs;
2. their action achieves their goals and ours;
3. this achievement satisfies both their needs and ours.

Identifying motivations and needs

Most people make the mistake of assuming that our personal motivations are universal: 'What motivates me must motivate the other person.' Not so. You may strike lucky— yes, they are motivated by the same things that you are. In fact, values, beliefs, needs and wants are far more complex than we tend to think. We are all driven by those things we regard as important in our lives. These might include a house of our own, a healthy bank balance, a loving relationship, praise and appreciation from those we look up to, and so on. Some people are driven by what might be regarded as negative motivations: greed, envy, fear. Although negative these drives are every bit as powerful as positive motivators.

Twenty basic human motivations

☺ Recognition
☺ Security
☺ Convenience
☺ Saving
☺ Profit
☺ Health
☺ Appetite
☺ Education
☺ Greed*
☺ Fear*

☺ Self-approval
☺ Culture
☺ Fashion
☺ Religion
☺ Love/affection
☺ Compassion
☺ Enjoyment
☺ Comfort
☺ Vanity*
☺ Sex*

* These needs can also be weaknesses. It is questionable to exploit these in others for the sake of influencing change—unless of course you can convince yourself that the change brought about will have a positive outcome or that these needs are in themselves positive.

To influence others we need to understand as much as we can about their motivations. What do they see as important considerations? What might they dislike? Broadly speaking motivators can be subdivided into:

- values
- beliefs
- needs
- wants.

Some people are better than others at observing behaviours and identifying what motivates them. Others base their judgements on a 'gut feel' which is often unreliable. There are three simple ways to understand what motivates others:

1. Observe for ourselves, conclude and verify our conclusions.
2. Ask the other person what motivates them (not as daft as it sounds). Observe what they tell you and verify its truth.
3. Ask someone else—a person who knows the individual concerned and has had sufficient relevant experience on which to base reliable judgement. Once again—observe and verify.

Values

Values are determined by who you want to be. They vary so much from person to person that there can be no hard and fast 'rules'. Values might include some of the following:

Honesty Faithfulness Integrity Achievement Love Independence Self-esteem Self-belief Self-confidence Success

These can be ranked in some arbitrary order. For example, a person may rank integrity and honesty higher than success. Or self-confidence over achievement.

In influencing there are three main points to bear in mind:

1. Knowing the other person's values may be of critical importance when the time comes to work out your strategy. If they place integrity high in their hierarchy of values and you make proposals which might compromise that value, you will fail.
2. Values tend to persist. They are formed over time. Perhaps they spring from the other person's upbringing. Maybe they form part of religious or philosophical teaching. Possibly the values are derived from a specially influential relationship.
3. Values can be so rooted in a person's psyche that it will almost certainly be counter-productive to try to shift them.

There is a well-known saying which neatly sums this up: in matters of principle, stand firm like a rock. In matters of opinion, flow like a river.

How we are controlled by our beliefs and opinions

Beliefs and opinions are commonly confused with values. The two are very different. While a value is usually deeply rooted and difficult to remove, beliefs can ebb and flow throughout a person's life. They are in a constant state of flux. Set firm today, challenged tomorrow. Learned at school, changed within months of leaving. Told by a trusted friend, later dismissed as nonsense. You will remember when you used to believe in Father Christmas, in the Tooth Fairy, in giants.

Here are some examples of universal beliefs:

My country/religion/team is the best.
All salespeople are out to con the customer.
Politicians are not to be believed.
Certain makes of car/washing machine/watch are more reliable than others.

Exercise—Understanding your values and beliefs

To understand how other people's values and beliefs may affect the way in which they are influenced take a few minutes now to examine your own. Notice how they affect the ways in which you make decisions.

1. List the five values which you regard as most important. At the same time remember how you came to hold these values. Where did the influence come from? Your parents? School? Religion? Relations? Friends? Neighbours? Society?

Continued

☐

☐

☐

2. Now note three beliefs you once held which you no longer regard as true. At the same time note what or who influenced your change of mind.

☐

☐

☐

Understanding your values and beliefs and why you would be prepared to have them changed puts you in a far better position to think about how you approach influencing others.

Needs

Much has been written about needs and what motivates human beings. For the purposes of influence it can be argued that there is little sense in wasting time distinguishing between a *need* and a *want*. Whether a person insists that they have a real need that remains unsatisfied, or that they simply want something, is academic. All we have to do is fulfil the requirement.

Here are some standard needs:

To save money	To gain a discount
To avoid spending money	To be seen to make the
To save time	'right' decision
To save effort	To meet a specification
To assert oneself	To be superior
To be secure	To defend/preserve
To be independent	To discover
To act	To conquer
To make more money	

And some wants:

To be first	To gain something for
To win a negotiation	nothing
To have the cheapest	To have the most expensive
solution	solution
To be different	To be envied
To be liked	To be comfortable
To possess or collect	To feel pleased and happy
To imitate and identify	To do nothing
To have the best	

You may have noticed that while the needs are tangible and measurable, the wants tend to be subjective. In other words, if a person thinks they have the best or cheapest solution, then they do. But don't discount wants simply because they are difficult to measure. They can be more powerful than the more tangible and objective needs.

Exercise—Needs analysis

To gain the most from this exercise it is helpful if you have a real example or case study to work with. If not, create a hypothetical example.

1. Think of a future situation where you want to influence a person or people. Decide on your objective and write it down.

2. Put yourself in the other person's shoes. Imagine that you are the one who will be making the decision to say 'yes' or 'no' to the proposition.

3. What are the most important or significant needs which you want fulfilling?

   ❑

   ❑

   ❑

Continued

4. Beyond the needs, is there anything that you or others would want? Be imaginative, try to avoid being influenced by your own set of criteria. This is an exercise in creative speculation. Speculate, creatively!
    ❏
    ❏

Using winning words

Throughout your future influencing dialogue with others you will, of course, be using words. Whether face-to-face at a meeting or presentation, one-to-one, over the telephone or in writing, the words you use will have an enormous bearing on your success.

Understand the needs of others and you will understand which words can transform a mundane suggestion into an irresistible invitation. Take a few tips from the experts in extracting the right response—the direct mail and mail order companies. They live or die by their abilities to influence our buying decisions. All of us are bombarded by junk mail, so what is it that separates the letters from successful mail order companies (such as Reader's Digest) from those that we throw away without even opening?

Now you can discover the easy-to-learn secrets of 'power words'

Top presenters, speakers, teachers and trainers use the words *you*, *we* and *I* extensively. They include the audience at all times in what they are saying or doing. For instance, 'You and I both know that this makes sense, don't we?' enrols the audience into the assumption that what is being suggested *does* make sense.

A number of words in the English language have been

identified as being more powerful than others. They are words which are more likely to stimulate a response in us when we hear or read them. They are words which have a magnetic attraction for all of us.

Yale University studied 'power words' and concluded that the most effective words were those which affect us most directly. Some examples include:

You/yours	Easy	Love	Free	Positive
Power	Save	Discover	Health	Success
Will	Greatest	Proven	Results	New
Guaranteed	Safe	Most	Best	Power
Pleased	When	Tested	Unique	Excellence
How to	Announcing	Now	Win	I wonder if

With your new list of words you have proven success tips that are easy to use. You will find yourself using these winning words in future influencing situations with positive results.

You and *yours* are the most powerful words you can use when influencing others. This is because they appeal directly and unequivocally to the individual or group. There is no doubt about it—your proposal or idea is aimed at *them*.

(The introductory section of this book uses the words you/your/yourself nearly sixty times.)

Summary

1. If you want to influence others to change ask 'How can I motivate them? What are their needs?'
2. Motivation is a forward-looking process, starting with needs. Needs create action, action achieves goals, achieving goals satisfies needs.
3. Human values, beliefs, needs and wants are complex. They change with time and outside influence.
4. Values are formed over time. It may be time-consuming or counter-productive to try to shift them.
5. Beliefs can be transitory and often ebb and flow throughout our lives.

6. Needs are usually tangible, wants are frequently subjective and can therefore represent more powerful motivations.
7. Using power words will add weight to your motivational statements.

Chapter 3

Asking the right questions

I only ask for information. Charles Dickens

Discovering the precise needs and wants of others is not always easy. This chapter explores various ways of identifying other people's requirements. As well as providing a résumé of basic question techniques, we reveal the power of SuperQuestions and the importance of becoming a good listener.

Let's suppose that you want to convince a friend to join you for a short holiday. Frankly, you need a break. Work has been very demanding lately and you know that a few days away will do you the world of good. You have seen an advertisement for a small country hotel. It is not expensive and has a reputation for French food. It is far enough away to provide variety but not too far to travel. You obtain a brochure and decide to tell your friend all about your exciting idea.

You are very surprised when your friend turns down your proposal. You cannot understand why he/she does not see the benefits. You feel rejected and dejected. But had you taken the trouble to check a few points before making your proposal perhaps your ideas would have met with more success.

Exercise—Planning to influence; an exercise in empathy

1. Using the example above (the proposed weekend break with a friend) or an example of your own, imagine that you are the person to be influenced. Sit back, shut your eyes and put yourself in their shoes.
2. Ask yourself what criteria would have to be met if you were to agree to a weekend break with a friend. Think of headings with which you could develop a simple checklist. Here are some to start with—you add to the list.

   ❑　Hotel

   ❑　Location

   ❑　Things to do

   ❑　Food I like

   ❑

   ❑

3. This analysis will confirm either that you are on the right lines and will be able to convince your friend, or that you may have to make some changes to your proposals.

Put yourself in the shoes of the person who is to be persuaded. Questions which you may want to ask yourself could include: Do you need a holiday right now? Do you like short holiday breaks? What do you think of country hotels? Which do you prefer—small or large hotels? What can you afford? Which parts of the country appeal to you? Do you have any special dietary requirements?

You must establish as early as you can whether the other person feels that they need what you are proposing. Plan-

ning and preparation will answer many of your questions—
but not all. Be warned—much time spent attempting to
influence can be wasted by failing to ask yourself quite basic
questions at the start.

Will I be wasting my time?

Your intentions may be sound, your proposition watertight—but can the other person say 'yes'? Do they have the
resources, the time, the will? Professional influencers set
great store by what is called 'pre-call planning'. It can be
time well spent and a worthwhile investment. It is impossible
to provide a list of dos and don'ts which will apply to all
circumstances; however, the following checklist should cover
most situations.

Before you begin to influence—a checklist

- ❏ Can this person make the decision to buy?
- ❏ Do I know or can I guess his/her needs?
- ❏ Are there any technical specifications which must be met?
- ❏ Are there any others whose influence may carry weight?
- ❏ Is there an intended time scale—yours or theirs?
- ❏ Is there a budget? How realistic is it?
- ❏ How will any costs be met?
- ❏ How do they typically make decisions?
- ❏ Does the thinking behind your proposition make sense?

How to ensure the best response from your questions

There is a story that sums up perfectly how a simple question
can transform our ability to influence people. When he saw
the sales receipt for over £70 000 the sales manager called
in the sales assistant concerned.

'Chris, this is the biggest single sale ever made by one of

our counter assistants. I want you to describe for me in detail, step by step, how you made the sale. Now, what was the first item the customer bought?'

'Twenty-five trout fishing hooks.'

'I see. What happened then?'

'I sold him some fishing line and reels, weights, wet and dry fishing flies and a rod and reel. Obviously he needed waders and waterproof clothing and a hat. I told him that it would be difficult carrying all that stuff so he would be better off with a permanent base to fish from. I sold him one of our pre-fabricated cabins. As the roads are pretty bad in the mountain regions I convinced him to buy a four-wheel-drive Jeep Cherokee. Oh, yes, then there was the boat and the trailer and the outboard motor.'

'This is amazing, Chris. You mean, this customer just came in asking for fish hooks and you sold him all these extras?'

'No, Mr Gresham. He didn't come in for fish hooks at all.'

'What did he come in for, then?'

'He just asked for directions to our maternity wear department so I said, "You look like being in for a rather boring time. Have you tried trout fishing?"'

One simple question which unlocked magnificent results. Most influencers use questions to discover useful information or to lead the other person towards a decision. This rather basic approach is limiting and can often fail. Here is an example:

Shop assistant: 'May I help you?'
Customer: 'No, thank you. I'm just looking.'

When will they ever learn? Over and over, day after day—same question, same response. Quite often a statement rather than a question will do the trick.

Shop assistant: 'Good afternoon. If you have any questions, just let me know. Please feel free to look around.'
Customer: 'Well, I was wondering if you have that colour in a size 42?'

or—

>Shop assistant: 'Good morning—those shirts are new in this week. What size are you looking for?'
>Customer: 'Have you a size 42?'

Categories of basic question

There is a wide variety of questions from which you can choose, depending on the desired outcome and response. Here are some examples.

1. Open questions

Any question starting with Who, What, How, Why, Where or When is likely to avoid a 'yes' or 'no' answer. Useful for probing and digging for deeper needs.
Example: 'How often does the problem arise?'; 'How important to you is a solution?'

2. Closed questions

Closed questions are used when you require a yes/no response, agreement or a short answer. As these questions obtain less information you may risk proceeding with less understanding of the other's needs.
Example: 'Shall we go ahead?'; 'Are you happy with that idea?'

3. Reflective questions

Reflective questions are generally based on the content of previous answers. They are psychologically powerful because they 'reflect' something the other person has said or feels and provide certain proof of your empathy and listening skills.
Example: 'Going back to your earlier point about performance; how important is that to you?'

4. Multiple questions

Several questions masquerading as a single question. A useful primer question to initiate dialogue but potentially confusing. Also the other person can choose which part of your multiple question to answer. Use with care and deliberation.

Example: 'What did you like about the job... was it the people, the location, the type of business or your manager...?'

5. Leading questions

Any question which *leads* the other person towards a response you wish or expect them to make. A form of questioning which many people resist. Use occasionally.

Example: 'You're not happy about that, are you?'

6. Assumptive questions

Such questions contain an assumption—therefore to disagree, the other person has to remove your assumption. Often, people will accept an assumption if it is prefaced with words such as: 'obviously'; 'clearly'; 'I'm sure you'll agree.'

Example: 'So you obviously agree with Mike's point of view?'

7. Add-on questions

Add-on questions are statements which have an additional phrase added to the end.

Examples: 'Reliability is an important consideration, isn't it?'; 'I am confident that will fit, don't you agree?'

Other add-ons include:

- Aren't they?
- Don't you?
- Couldn't it?

- Isn't that right?
- Shouldn't we?
- Don't you agree?

Add-on questions are similar to assumptive questions, but more subtle and powerful. You make an assumptive statement and add on phrases which are designed to encourage the listener to agree with your assertion. (I am sure that you recognize this category of question, don't you?).

8. Alternative choice questions

The salesperson's best friend. The so-called 'tea or coffee close'. This technique forces the other person to make a choice from what is offered. More powerful than asking: 'Do you like the red one?'
Example: 'Which of these two packaging designs do you prefer—the red one or the green one?'

9. Background questions

Background questions provide basic information from which you can draw conclusions.
Example: 'What was it that led Mike to make that decision?'

10. Problem questions

Problem questions begin to focus on the other person's situation, or problem.
Example: 'What kind of problems did that produce?' (Note the use of an open, assumptive, question. Asking 'Did that produce any problems?' would allow the other person to say 'No'.)

11. Effect questions

Effect questions define what is happening as a result of the prevailing situation, or problem.

Example: 'What will happen if nothing is done about that?'

12. Need questions

Need questions allow the person to state the requirements in their terms which will help reinforce their commitment to your proposed solutions, or suggestions.
Example: 'If you had that, how useful would it be to you in the future?'

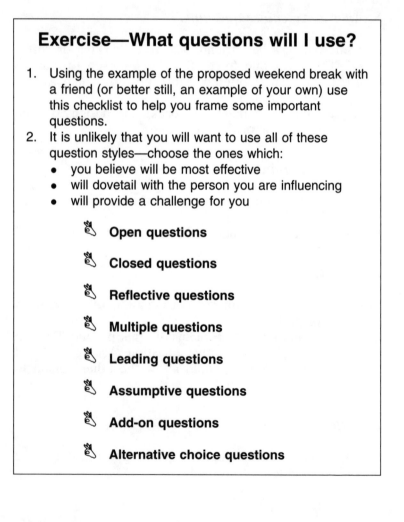

Exercise—What questions will I use?

1. Using the example of the proposed weekend break with a friend (or better still, an example of your own) use this checklist to help you frame some important questions.
2. It is unlikely that you will want to use all of these question styles—choose the ones which:
    *   you believe will be most effective
    *   will dovetail with the person you are influencing
    *   will provide a challenge for you

> **Open questions**
>
> **Closed questions**
>
> **Reflective questions**
>
> **Multiple questions**
>
> **Leading questions**
>
> **Assumptive questions**
>
> **Add-on questions**
>
> **Alternative choice questions**

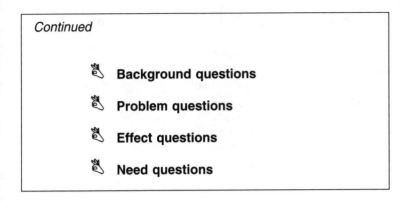

The SuperQuestion technique

Each of us uses our own language, based on personal experience. These experiences colour the meanings of our words and can result in communication ambiguity and misunderstandings. To be able fully to understand other people, we need also to be able to understand their ways of thinking. Each person's understanding of what goes on around them is their 'reality'. Curiously it may not be the same 'reality' that we understand. Have you ever been on a walk with a friend and noticed or heard or smelt different things? This is quite common. Ask two people to describe the bank robber and you could be looking for two robbers—their descriptions may be that different!

Reality—whatever that means—can only be described in words. Reality is what other people believe it to be. When we describe our version of reality we create our description from sensory-based language—what we saw, heard, touched, felt emotionally, smelt or tasted. That is it. We have no more ways of talking about our understanding. This is why communication can go so badly wrong.

All nouns can be divided into two categories:

- **specific; definite; concrete**
- **vague; abstract; nominalization**

Some examples of each 'type' (treated as nouns) are:

Specific	Vague
book	trust
silk	patriotism
path	quality
car	loyalty
nails	effectiveness
manager	worry
field	productivity
wall	profit

The dictionary defines 'friend' as 'a person for whom one feels affection; whom one knows intimately; companion; helper; colleague; associate; acquaintance'. Clearly, everyone has a different interpretation of the word 'friend'. Which friend, specifically? Who, exactly, do you mean? Precisely how friendly? What do you mean, specifically? Friendly under what circumstances?

If three people are discussing 'productivity' each could be using the word from a different perspective (perhaps associated with past experience or future expectations). 'Productivity—the rate at which something is produced,' declares the dictionary. Produced by what, specifically? People? Machines? Department? Company? Productivity of what?

If you want to discover what a person means, how thought processes affect behaviour, you need only to learn two sets of questions, which I call SuperQuestions. To take someone where you want to go you have to know where they are at the moment. To influence their ideas, you have to know what those ideas are. These SuperQuestions will become the most powerful and important you will ever learn.

Before we look at the SuperQuestions themselves, you will need to recognize the moment in a conversation when you will want to use one of these questions. Just as there are a number of questions to ask, there are also some signals which will enable you to use the appropriate SuperQuestion. The three moments when a SuperQuestion can release a communication blockage are:

- when a statement made by another person has information missing from it;
- when statements are made which contain apparent rules, limitations or generalizations;
- when statements are made which suggest a distorted view of reality.

The SuperQuestion technique

Some examples of ways in which you might hear a statement and detect the moment when a SuperQuestion will come to your rescue are given below. The examples given are brief, to help you learn the technique. In real life, however, it is often useful to soften the question. For example—'Oh, that's interesting . . .' 'I know what you mean . . .' 'That's a good point you've raised . . .' 'Can I just ask . . .' or simply repeat the statement back to them. The technique works best when there is good rapport and where each person wants to achieve the same outcome.

Missing information questions

Some people delete words on purpose. Sometimes a word is missed out altogether so that the meaning is incomplete or ambiguous. To make sense of the statement we need to recover the missing word.

Every parent will recognize this conversation which I had recently with my daughter:

Me: Where are you going?
Charlotte: Out to meet some friends.
Me: Who?
Charlotte: Don't know yet, depends on who turns up.
Me: Where are you meeting them?
Charlotte: In a pub.
Me: Which pub?
Charlotte: One in town.
Me: When are you getting back then?
Charlotte: Late.

Me: How late is 'late'?

Charlotte: After midnight?

Me: How long after midnight? When should I begin to worry about you?

Deliberate evasion is easy. Just leave out the facts, the specifics, the adjectives and adverbs. It is not always a matter of deliberate deception through evasion. Perhaps the other person knows their subject matter so thoroughly that they mistakenly believe that they have included certain pieces of important information.

The following are examples of statements which contain 'missing' or 'deleted' information, together with the Super-Question which should solve the 'riddle'.

Nouns which mean nothing to you—use a SuperQuestion

The following SuperQuestions elicit specific information about the noun used.

'I am going to the *shop*.'
'Which shop, specifically?'

'*Profits* are looking good this year.'
'Which profits, exactly?'

'I want a *new job*.'
'What job, precisely?'

'*They* don't listen to me.'
'Who is it specifically that doesn't listen to you?'

Notice how much more useful these questions are than 'What do you mean by ...?'

Imprecise verbs—use a SuperQuestion

The following questions recover specific information about the way a person is using a verb.

'My boss *annoyed* me.'
'How exactly did he annoy you?'

'Productivity is *falling*.'
'How specifically is productivity falling?'

'I am *frightened*.'
'What exactly is frightening you?'

Verbs which have been turned into vague nouns. Use a SuperQuestion

These are known as nominalizations—nouns which may mean something to the speaker but whose meaning is unclear to others.

'I want *recognition*.'
'How, specifically, do you want to be recognized?'

'She wants a better *education*.'
'What exactly does she mean by education?'

'Job *satisfaction* is important to him.'
'In what ways does he want to feel satisfied?'

The above questions recover the changed verb process and enable us to consider the person's interpretation of the 'nominalization'.

Unspecified comparisons—use a SuperQuestion

The following questions will help you to discover the standard of the comparison which is being made.

'This is the *nicest* model.'
'Nicer than what, exactly?' or **'In what specific ways is it nice?'**

'She's the *best* person for the job.'
'Better than whom, specifically?'

'This product is *cheapest.*'
'Cheaper than what, specifically?'

Apparent rules, limitations and generalization—use a SuperQuestion

The following questions probe limits which are placed on actions or thoughts. They examine people's value judgements. They challenge perceived rules and exceptions.

'You *mustn't* do it that way.'
'What would happen if I did?'

'We *should* always keep a copy.'
'What would happen if we didn't keep copies?'

'We *must* publish the financial report by the 15th.'
'What would happen if we were later than that?'

'I *can't* do that.'
'I can understand your difficulty but what exactly is preventing you from doing it?'

'We *never* promote people in their first two years.'
'Was there ever a time when you did promote someone earlier than that?'

'*Everybody* should seek further education.'
'Everybody . . . ?'

'That's *not possible.*'
'What would have to happen to make it possible?'

NB. Use these questions with some care as they could cause trouble ('You can't have an extra day off'—'What would happen if I did?' could well infuriate your boss! Try instead 'What would have to happen for me to have that day off?' or 'What's preventing you from allowing me?')

Notice what happens when you use rules, limitations and generalization questions on yourself, to challenge your own preconceived ideas and thinking processes.

When people's thinking distorts reality—use a SuperQuestion

The following questions explore and reform distortions in people's perception of the world. For example, a *distortion* is where X is assumed automatically to lead to Y; value judgements, rules and opinions in which the source of the assertion is missing; assuming you know what someone is thinking or feeling; belief that one person's action can cause another's emotional reaction, rather than simply inviting it.

'It's *wrong* to think like that.'
'How do you know it is wrong?'

'We can't buy another policy *because* it will cost too much.'
'How would having another policy cost you too much?'

'People like that *annoy me*'.
'How do people like that annoy you?'

'That's professionally presented, *so* it's bound to be expensive.'
'How does it being professionally presented mean that it's bound to be expensive?'

'*You don't understand* what I'm saying.'
'What leads you to believe that I don't understand you?'

Softening your SuperQuestions

The effect that all of these questions may have on others can be alarming. You are asking them to see things from a new or different perspective; for some people this process can be both difficult and annoying. Think carefully about your motives—will the use of these questions clarify language to the advantage of both parties? If the words used by the other person are unimportant to the outcome of the dialogue, don't bother to use the SuperQuestion technique.

When you have developed your skills in SuperQuestioning and have been doing this subconsciously for a while, begin to notice what signs occur which let you know that you are successfully distinguishing other people's use of language and the right moment to use a SuperQuestion.

How to improve your listening skills

The value of becoming a superior listener cannot be stressed too much. Watching others in social situations will show how most people listen most of the time. Much of our 'listening time' is devoted to trying to re-enter the conversation, thinking out our next statement or argument, looking away from the speaker and noticing our surroundings. Some simple (even obvious) suggestions for improving listening skills are detailed below.

Eye contact

Never take your eyes off any person who is speaking. Even if they are not directing their speech at you it is still important to look at them. Give your full attention and use the sensory information you get back to assist your interpretation of what's being said. Don't worry about 'staring out' the speaker. You will notice that most speakers don't look directly at the listener all of the time. If they do have a direct gaze, you can be confident that they won't worry too much if you have a level gaze as well.

Body language

Use your posture and gestures to signal that you are listening. There are no 'rules' to follow—just be natural. Many people find that leaning forward—towards the speaker—is preferable to leaning back or away. A hand cupped around the chin, forefinger vertically up the cheek and head tilted slightly often suggests rapt attention. Tilt your head to left or right and you will signal your concern and empathy. Give plenty of nods and appropriate facial expressions to confirm that you are listening.

Noises off

Given that most speakers do not look continuously at their listener, a few sounds and short phrases can enhance the listening process. Examples: 'I see'; 'Uh huh'; 'Oh really?'; 'Did you?'; 'So what happened then?' Laughter or appropriate sounds suggesting amazement, sympathy and so on will help propel the speaker during the short periods when they are not looking at you.

Reflective questions

Reflective questions are powerful signals which prove beyond doubt that you are listening carefully—it is impossible to use reflective questions without listening. These questions spring from previous information gained from the speaker's conversation content and contain the speaker's words and phrases, even intonation.

Language patterns

The effective listener will recognize that the speaker uses certain language patterns (e.g. 'I'm really fed up with this guy') or technical terminology. Noticing this, the effective listener will use the same language in their responses:
   'What is it that is making you fed up with this guy?'

Exercise—How to listen

1. Begin to notice how you listen. What makes you listen more actively? What kind of distractions prevent you from concentrating? Do you use a particular style or type of listening? Do you listen differently with people you know or like? Is your style different with customers? Colleagues? Management? Partner?

2. Experiment with not listening! Notice the effect it has on others. Do this in face-to-face conversations as well as on the telephone.

3. Practise matching your voice with other people's. Speak as they do—fast, slow, loud, soft. Notice their tone of voice and match it. Notice what happens to their voice when you alter your voice tone.

4. Be aware of the content of conversation. Notice the jargon and language patterns the other person uses. See what happens if you mismatch these patterns. What happens if you match the patterns?

Summary

1. Think through your proposition. Invest time in planning. Put yourself in the other person's shoes.
2. In face-to-face or telephone communication, questions are your most valuable tool.
3. Learn as many question styles as you can. Notice which are more, or less, productive and the ways in which people respond.
4. Learn to use SuperQuestions: when information is missing, when people respond with apparent rules, limitation statements or generalizations or when reality is distorted.
5. Learn to soften your SuperQuestions. And only use them when they are really needed.

6.   Improve your listening skills through good eye contact, congruent body language and noises off. The use of reflective questions will also indicate that you are listening intently.

Chapter 4

Matching your ideas to their needs

I love strawberries, but when I go fishing I bait my hook with worms. Dale Carnegie

So, what's in it for the other person? This chapter shows you how to dovetail your message with the other person's values and needs.

In a previous chapter we saw how people are motivated by their values and beliefs as well as more specific needs and wants. Probably the biggest single weakness demonstrated by salespeople is:

They don't match benefits to needs

Recently a friend called David wanted to change his car. For years he had been driving company cars, mainly Fords. Now he had become self-employed he thought the time had arrived when he should make some changes. He looked around and finally plumped for Volvo. One Saturday morning David headed for the local Volvo showroom and was looking around when a saleswoman approached him. The dialogue went something like this:

Saleswoman: 'Good morning, my name is Michelle. Are

you looking for something specific or just seeing what we have to offer?'

David: 'Hello, I'm David Ball. I want to change my car so thought I would come in and see what you have available.'

Michelle: 'Why don't we sit down, Mr Ball, and you can tell me a bit more about your requirements. By the way, would you like a coffee or would you prefer tea?' (Fetches coffee in thin plastic cups which take a good ten minutes to drink as they are so hot to handle!)

Michelle: 'What sort of car do you drive at present, Mr Ball?'

David: 'A two-litre Ford saloon, a company car.'

Michelle: 'I see. And what sort of driving do you use it for mainly? Is it city or country, motorways or smaller roads, business or pleasure?'

David: 'Mainly business on motorways. I do about 40 000 kilometres a year. I also use the car for holidays.'

Michelle: 'I get the picture. Tell me, Mr Ball, how many passengers do you usually carry and where do you go on holiday?'

David: 'It's usually my wife and two teenage children. We generally rent a property abroad so we have a fairly full car.'

Michelle: 'And which is more important to you—safety or fuel consumption?'

David: 'Definitely safety. I have the family to think about and I carry around a lot of bulky and valuable equipment. I can claim most of my petrol expenses on my company account.'

Michelle: 'I see. How about reliability? How important is that to you?'

David: 'Probably the most important single consideration. I am a self-employed consultant and have very strict deadlines to meet. I do not want to be worrying all the time about breaking down. I'd say reliability and safety are my chief concerns.'

The conversation continued in this fashion for a little longer then Michelle suggested they look at a particular car.

Michelle: 'I believe this is the car for you, Mr Ball. It is an estate, so you can easily load that bulky equipment. It also gives you plenty of extra space for those long trips abroad with the family. Safety and reliability are the hall-marks of Volvo, which are regarded by most people as the leaders in this field. As we recommend frequent servicing this helps to avoid future problems as we replace parts before they become a problem.'

This example shows how two influencing skills can be put to work in conjunction with one another. The first is a detailed fact find which probes and analyses requirements (did you spot the values, the beliefs, the needs and the wants?). The second skill is showing how the benefits of the proposal dovetail with the needs.

What's in it for me?

How many times have you been at a meeting or a presentation where the speaker rambles on and on about the specific details when all you want to hear is 'What is in it for me?' The problem is simple. Most of us can become very excited about an idea or a project. We live, sleep and eat it. So when the time comes to tell others all about it we overdo the detail. I remember once buying a radio. It was just what I wanted but the sales assistant insisted on taking the back off the set in order to show me all the exciting electronic components it contained. He was a fan of all things electronic. These shiny bits and bobs really excited his imagination. I could not fault his enthusiasm—it simply did not ignite mine. I couldn't care less about the innards. All I wanted to know was: 'Will it receive the BBC in South East Asia? If so, I'll have it.'

This common problem can easily be corrected. At its core lies the blurred distinction between a feature of the item or idea, the benefits those features provide and any advantages it has when compared with alternative courses of action.

How to distinguish between benefits, features and advantages

Every time you attempt to influence or persuade someone you will be stressing benefits, features and advantages. You can't avoid it. They are the building blocks of your persuasive case. Each is in its way valuable. They all add credence to your message. But they do not carry the same value. If we scaled the three building blocks in order of value it would look like this:

1. Benefits—highly potent whenever they actually fulfil perceived needs and wants.
2. Features—potentially boring and unnecessary unless the other person requires proof or evidence or loves all the technical information.
3. Advantages—useful but possibly dangerous as they usually include comparisons with alternative courses of action.

To really understand the value and potency of benefits, features and advantages we need some definitions.

How to identify features—example

Imagine that you are Facilities Manager for a medium-sized engineering company. Let's take a closer look at benefits, features and advantages and how each may be used to develop an appropriate argument with which to convince your Directors. There are two factory buildings on site, one containing 45 workers, the other 32 workers. At present tea or coffee is brewed twice a day in a central kitchen. There is a hot water boiler, a sink, cupboards for provisions and shelves where cups and mugs are stored. Each section (about eight workers) takes a morning and afternoon break, staggered to avoid clashing with other sections. One person is allocated the task of making tea or coffee for his or her section for one week.

You have been approached by a vending machine company. They can see many flaws in your current system:

- time wasting (dispensing; washing up);
- unhygienic (cracked mugs; poor washing up);
- dangerous (breakages);
- morale (workers tied down to fixed break times);
- money wasting (in terms of time spent; ingredients used; utensils).

You agree with their arguments and feel that you can use them to convince your Directors to make the switch. The vending machine company is proposing the installation of four suitably located vending machines. Each would dispense a variety of beverages 24 hours a day. Drinks would be delivered in the familiar plastic cups, ribbed sides, conical, coffee coloured.

Let's examine the eight main **features** of these plastic cups:

1. 1p per cup
2. 10 cm high
3. conical shape
4. made from plastic
5. coffee coloured
6. ribbed sides
7. disposable
8. produced locally

These features are technical aspects. Even if the Directors do not agree with your proposals to install vending machines, these technical features will remain true of the plastic cups.

Only after agreeing to go ahead will the features become **benefits**. It is impossible to benefit from anything until you acquire it, use it, read it, see it—and so on. The problem with most salespeople (and untrained influencers!) is that they are so familiar with the features of their proposal that they forget to translate them into attractive benefits for the other person.

Translating features into benefits

Knowing all the features of your proposition or idea is important. You may be asked to prove your claims, and features are a way of validating your conclusions—a form of proof. Even more important is the ability to avoid talking about them. The only thing which will excite the other person's imagination is the answer to the age-old question: 'What's in it for me?' In other words, how will I benefit from your idea? How do the benefits dovetail with my perceived needs?

If you do need to mention features then also point out the attendant benefit in the same breath. For example:

'These cups are made from plastic (product feature) *which means that* they are more hygienic than mugs and will cut down sickness and absenteeism (benefit)'; or 'These plastic cups are conical in shape (product feature) *which means that* they can be stacked and will save considerable storage space (benefit)'.

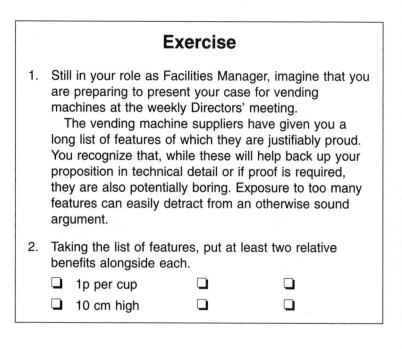

Exercise

1.   Still in your role as Facilities Manager, imagine that you are preparing to present your case for vending machines at the weekly Directors' meeting.

   The vending machine suppliers have given you a long list of features of which they are justifiably proud. You recognize that, while these will help back up your proposition in technical detail or if proof is required, they are also potentially boring. Exposure to too many features can easily detract from an otherwise sound argument.

2.   Taking the list of features, put at least two relative benefits alongside each.

   ❑ 1p per cup   ❑   ❑
   ❑ 10 cm high   ❑   ❑

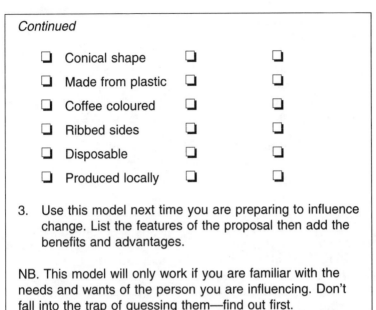

Continued

❏ Conical shape ❏ ❏
❏ Made from plastic ❏ ❏
❏ Coffee coloured ❏ ❏
❏ Ribbed sides ❏ ❏
❏ Disposable ❏ ❏
❏ Produced locally ❏ ❏

3. Use this model next time you are preparing to influence change. List the features of the proposal then add the benefits and advantages.

NB. This model will only work if you are familiar with the needs and wants of the person you are influencing. Don't fall into the trap of guessing them—find out first.

The dangers of advantages

First of all—what do we mean by an 'advantage'? A thesaurus might put it like this:

> *advantage*, head start, lead, edge, upper hand, trump card, ace up one's sleeve, leverage, clout.

Your proposition includes additional features and benefits when compared to an alternative proposition. You are suggesting a new way of doing things, a different approach. But there is an alternative. Will the other person prefer the alternative? Is this something they are familiar with, happy with, comfortable with? Even if your proposal is:

- cheaper
- faster
- easier

- an improvement
- smaller
- larger
- less distance away
- guaranteed
- more accessible
- more popular,

there is no certainty that it will achieve universal acclaim.

Why not? It has so many advantages to offer, surely it cannot fail? There are several possible reasons:

1. They are happy with the present situation. 'Why change just for the sake of it? We might find ourselves going from the frying pan into the fire.' Perhaps there is some kind of 'deal' which obliges them to remain as they are.
2. They agree with everything you say but everything you say contrasts rather too favourably with earlier decisions which they made. Why didn't they do what you are suggesting the first time round? What will their boss or partner think if they suddenly switch horses in midstream? Won't their judgement be called into question? Better to stay as we are, thanks all the same.
3. Unconvinced of the final dividends. 'OK, so we'll save effort and worry—but for £45 000? No, thanks!' or 'Sure the cost will rise if I don't make a decision to go ahead. All the more reason to stay as I am.'
4. Too much trouble. 'It's just not worth the bother which change would involve.'
5. Sheer cussedness. 'I realize you have some good points to make—but I just don't want to change. That's that. Sorry.'

The way in which you disclose your advantages can determine your eventual level of success. Phrases which antagonize people include:

'I can't see why you persist with the old system when mine is so much better.'
'Just think of all the time you'll save.'

'That way of doing things is from the Dark Ages. You need to modernize, enter the twenty-first century.'
'Everyone else is doing it this way—you'll see the light sooner or later.'

Don't fall into the trap of thinking that these comments are so crass as to be laughable: I have heard every one of these statements made. Each is intended to shift the other person's perceptions, to encourage them to reconsider old beliefs. But all they succeed in producing is an even more determined attempt to support old ideas—even if these are patently insupportable. In other words: 'I know what you say makes sense but I'll stick with what I have if you don't mind.'

How to present the advantages of your suggestion

Think carefully before you present the advantages of your ideas. You will be making comparisons with other possible solutions, including 'do nothing'. If you are to avoid other people digging in their heels and refusing to budge (even when they know you are correct), you must phrase your advantage statements very carefully. Here are some suggestions you might like to try next time you need to be more successful at convincing someone of the advantages of your proposal. You will notice that both questions force the other person to examine the possibilities of beneficial success.

- 'If you were to save even more time by doing it this way, how exactly could that benefit your department?'
- 'What would have to happen for you to test my claims over a three-month period to check for yourselves that the additional savings are worth having?'

A further method of proving advantages is by encouraging others to check the validity of your assertions. 'Joe didn't believe the advantages so I suggested he called Julia to check for himself. Why not give her a call yourself?'

Exercise

1. You are about to go into the weekly Directors' meeting. You are fully aware of the features and benefits which your proposal will offer. The Directors are concerned about the time spent making tea and coffee. They also think that current methods of storage and washing up are possibly unhygienic.
2. What advantages will the installation of vending machines bring?
3. List the three main advantages.

4. How will you present these to the Directors? Write down the phrases which you will use.

Summary

1. The successful influencer fully understands the distinctions between a benefit, a feature and an advantage and uses each at the right moment.
2. Benefits are anything which fulfil needs and wants.
3. Features are technical details which may meet needs and provide proof.
4. Advantages are additional benefits which your proposition confers when compared to alternative propositions.
5. The overuse of advantages can create a backlash. People may dig their heels in, supporting previous decisions even if these are insupportable.

Chapter 5

Developing the relationship

Two-thirds of all European business deals worth more than £6.5 million are agreed over a game of golf. Source: the German economics magazine, *Kapital*

A major factor in influencing others is how well you interact with them. This chapter examines the ways in which relationships develop and how this process can be used to improve and maintain your success as an influencer.

Close to where I live there are two pubs. One sells very good beers and cider, the other is 'tied' to a brewer and obliged to sell that brewer's proprietary brands. The people who run the tied house are generous, helpful and very friendly. Which is why I drink there, rather than at the pub which sells the better beer. So what is it that influences my decision? Good beer? Or the people who run the pub? Most of us base decisions of this sort on the people factor. If we like the people, we'll buy. If we don't like the people— forget it. Even if it causes us some inconvenience we will find someone we *do* like—and give them the business.

So—if people do buy people, how easy will it be to isolate people factors which may be important to consider when trying to influence others? It is at once easy and difficult.

Easy because all of us are able to interact with some people better than others. Difficult because most of us do not bother to analyse the reasons why we do or don't have a harmonious relationship. If we did stop for a moment to study our evaluative processes we would discover that it all reduces to one thing—rapport.

Rapport is the lubricant of all human communication. It is the ultimate influencing skill, more important than our knowledge of our subject, awareness of our 'market', or ability to persuade. Good rapport oils the wheels of the many communications we have with other human beings. From the moment we leave our bed to the time our head hits the pillow once more, most of us are in almost perpetual contact with other people. And, without rapport to smooth the interface of daily communication, many opportunities to influence can be lost.

It has been calculated that the average person has no more than half a dozen friends on earth. Not acquaintances—real friends. You don't believe it? Stop now, find a piece of paper and start listing your friends. (A friend is someone on whom you could rely totally in times of real crisis; someone who would lend you money and give you space in their home for an indefinite period.) How did you do? If you listed more than six, count yourself lucky—you are doing well for friends in your life.

Friends are usually those people with whom you have the greatest rapport. A harmonious relationship where you immediately feel comfortable. No special behaviour is required from you or them. No posturing or wariness is necessary—every time you meet one another you both dive deep into an engaging and enduring partnership with ease and joy. Time has worn away the rough edges of your early relationship. Like favourite clothes, or a comfortable chair, your real friendships require no 'wearing in' period.

Wouldn't it be great if you could slip as easily into all your social and business relationships? Just think how rich you would be—materially and spiritually—if all the people you have to persuade, convince, influence and interact with were as comfortable to be with as your own friends. It is possible to develop early and long-lasting rapport with others with remarkably little effort. All you need is to understand exactly what makes some of your personal relationships so successful, and transfer these natural skills to all other relationships. A complete awareness of your own natural social skills will give you the power to transfer these skills straight into any relationship. Before we break down these instinctive techniques of yours into digestible chunks for further learning, let's examine some basic areas of business (and social) communication which may require the lubrication of rapport.

It is easier to influence change in others if you:

- are able to form strong, long-lasting relationships easily and quickly;
- understand how your personality dovetails with others;
- are aware of and use elementary non-verbal communication.

Forming strong relationships

How many times have you walked into a room full of strangers and made immediate judgements about them? Which one do I like? Who am I most likely to feel comfortable with? Who is the most desirable person here? My guess is that most of us do this, most of the time. It's only human, after all. We make decisions about the rest of humanity based on our unerring ability to read people like a book!!

At first, all goes according to plan. We circle around one another forming the first steps in the dance of rapport. Perhaps the other person knows the same moves—and, for a while, we circle together in a simple two-step. But then the tune changes or others want to join in. We discover that our first impression was incorrect. Maybe just slightly wrong; sometimes totally wrong.

This is a common phenomenon. The reason we make many misjudgements about other people is because, in the formation phase of a relationship, people often make allowances for each other in order to develop the relationship faster. You have just met someone for the first time. You strike up a conversation and soon discover you like this person. They seem to like your company, too. You chat about that play you both saw on TV last night—the play you thought was the best you have seen for a long time. It turns out that your new acquaintance thought the play was poorly written and badly acted. 'Yes', you find yourself half agreeing, 'it wasn't that well acted and maybe the writing was a little flat at times'.

Only moments into the relationship and you have already prepared to tone down some beliefs and attitudes. You are modifying more radical ideas, suppressing some of your wilder thoughts. It is quite common for people to do this— in order to keep the relationship on track during its delicate formation phase. But, do you always do this with people at work or new neighbours? Many people believe it is more important to have good relationships with people outside work than in business. Why should we have to adjust our cherished beliefs in front of this new customer? After all, we probably wouldn't choose to be with him/her in a social situation. The answer to this common dilemma is easy. You need never again compromise your position.

Suppose others say something you don't agree with. A political judgement, perhaps, or some negative comment about a third person. In future, instead of stating your case and risking conflict in the early formation phase of the relationship, learn to see things always from their point of view.

The more points of view you have, the better

The person in any complex communication who takes the greatest variety of possible viewpoints is in a better position to control the dialogue. To understand this concept, take as an example a typical home central heating system. A big, powerful boiler fired by gas, perhaps; plenty of radiators linked by a lengthy network of copper tubing; a hot water tank, one or two heated towel rails. What controls the system? The size of each radiator? The length of piping?

The gas pressure? None of these controls the system. The thermostat controls it. The smallest, but most flexible, 'thinking' part of the entire system is in charge.

Try looking at things from different points of view:

1. our own point of view;
2. the other person's viewpoint;
3. imagining how an outsider might see things.

It is all too easy to see things solely from our own point of view. From now on, you may find yourself saying things such as 'I can understand why you think that, Mr Garrison.' 'Hmmm. I see your point of view.' 'Yes, that's understandable.' When you do this, you will not be compromising—you will be empathizing.

Later, when you know a person better, you can and possibly should state your opinions more boldly. But avoid the temptation in the early formation phase, especially in a business relationship.

Long-term relationships go through three, and sometimes four, distinct phases:

- Formation
- Development
- Consolidation and further development on new levels of understanding
- Breakdown

As a flexible influencer you will naturally want to form strong relationships by reaching phase three, consolidation, as soon as you can—and keep the relationship there for as long as possible, without ever reaching the breakdown phase.

Developing and consolidating the business relationship

The formation of early business relationships is quite easy: follow two rules; remain flexible and avoid 'Yes—but ...'.

More work, much more effort, is required if you are to move into the development and consolidation phases of your new relationship.

Earlier, we learned how to apply our natural social skills to the formation phase of a new relationship. Now, you need to understand precisely what skills you employ which make your personal relationships flourish and survive the test of time. These skills, too, can be mapped on to all business relationships. Although most of us have developed a variety of ways which help us to interact with others, there are three principal techniques for developing and consolidating your relationships:

- meeting frequently;
- being prepared to self-disclose;
- discovering things you have in common.

Meeting frequently

My wife and I have some very good friends who live on the other side of the country, a six-hour drive away. We don't see one another very often—once or twice a year, at most. Last time we met, Jane and Pete observed how our relationship was always 'so easy to pick up where we left off last time'. They went on to point out that 'we have a seamless conversation which carries on, uninterrupted, down the years'. However, the reality is very different. Our relationship has actually stood still.

Pete and Jane have changed over the years we have known them—so have my wife and I. Events, growth and development, even death, have all had an impact on our separate lives. When we meet on one of our infrequent encounters, these influential events have not been shared— we are unaware of how each of our lives has been affected in the intervening time we have spent apart. We have not grown alongside one another, we have literally grown apart. We have less and less in common. We lead separate existences. The couple we travel all that distance to see have become different people. Our relationship is teetering on the edge of breakdown.

Clearly, the more opportunity you have to meet others the greater will be the chances of developing a lasting relationship. You will constantly be tuned in to their ever-changing business needs; better able to react swiftly to these altered circumstances with appropriate suggestions. Familiarity need not necessarily breed contempt. Well-adjusted adults tend to be able to adapt well to one another.

One of my clients, a life insurance company, sell their products through a broker network. Recently, I was talking to one of their brokers, tied exclusively to my client, and asked her 'What made you choose Osborne Life?' Without hesitation she replied, 'Gary. He was the reason I chose Osborne.' Intrigued, I quizzed her further. 'So what was it Gary did that impressed you most?' The broker paused, then smiled widely. 'It wasn't what he did as much as what he didn't do. He didn't give up.' She went on, 'The first time I met him, I was quite rude to him and told him to leave my office. The second time, he stayed a bit longer and we talked for a while. Not about Osborne Life Assurance— about my business, the economy and so on. We discovered we both played squash at the same sports centre. We knew some of the same people. But I still told him not to bother me further as I was quite happy with the business arrangement I had with another life assurance company.'

I gently pressed her for more information. 'He obviously didn't stay away?' 'No', she replied, 'he didn't.' Apparently, two weeks later she went into her outer office and discovered Gary sitting there, talking to one of the clerical assistants. It seems that Gary had discovered that the assistant was unsure of a recent change in financial services legislation and he was talking her through it. Noticing this, the broker asked him to step inside her office. 'Later, Gary told me that he was frightened that I was about to reprimand him for pestering my staff. Instead, we talked in detail about the Finance Services Act, his sales philosophy and, inevitably, Osborne Life Assurance. The rest is history. When I decided to switch companies, I didn't buy Osborne Life Assurance—I bought Gary.'

So, persistence does pay off, after all. As the relationship consolidates, influencing others becomes quite natural and no pressure is needed.

Self-disclosure

Most of us like people who are like ourselves. We swarm, flock and group together by type, background, interests, beliefs, gender, work and so on. But how do we find out enough about other people to decide whether we want to be in their company in the first place?

We self-disclose. Most developing relationships reach a point at which one or other party feels the urge to reveal aspects of their life or themselves to the other person. This can happen verbally as in 'I am off on holiday at the end of the week', which invites the response, 'Oh, really? Where are you going?' More subtly, one statement tucked into another can evoke a self-disclosure response. 'A few years ago, when I worked in the retail trade . . .' ('I didn't know you were in retailing. When was that . . .?')

Perhaps you wear a special tie (old school?) or a badge or pin which shows that you are a member of a club, have some special interest or religious belief. If so, you are self-disclosing.

You may now find yourself noticing 'self-disclosure' in the future, and discovering that it frequently leads on to . . .

Biographic matching

We have already learned that many people feel an affiliation with others who are in some way like themselves. This is a small part of what is known as 'matching'. It is rare for people who have little in common to congregate in each other's company for long. Mutual interests, ideas, values and beliefs are the warp and weft of social interaction and they help bind us to one another. Easy enough in social circles but far more difficult when you find yourself confronted by a customer with a big budget—with whom you have absolutely nothing in common!

Because matching can be social or economic, achieved through outlook, education or background, it is rare for two human beings to avoid the compulsion to discover similarities about themselves. All of us love creating little compartments into which we can pop other people. Following some early self-disclosure, a typical matching conversation might go something like this:

You: 'You were saying that you are off for a long weekend in the Lake District. Do you manage to get away from the business very often?'

Them: 'No—this is the first time for about a year. Our daughter was born last March, so we feel we can go out and about a bit more, now.'

You: 'We have a 6-month-old son and know the feeling. Whereabouts in the Lake District are you staying?'

Them: 'Near Ullswater—do you know it?'

You: 'Yes, very well. A neighbour of ours has a cottage which she lets to one or two acquaintances.'

Them: 'I wouldn't mind her telephone number some time—we'd be very interested in renting a decent place next year.'

All this may sound unrealistic and contrived, but if you look back on conversations you have had with near strangers, real life is frequently more extraordinary than any conversation I can dream up. Recently, I was flying from London to Kuala Lumpur, via Singapore. On the London–Singapore leg of the journey I sat next to a woman who is employed by a client of mine in the UK. Naturally, we talked and found that we had much in common and, of course, discovered that we had several mutual acquaintances through her job. Some hours later, on the Singapore–Kuala Lumpur leg of my journey, I sat beside a man who turned out to be the Hong Kong Vice-president of one of the world's largest insurance groups. Sure enough, after only a few minutes' conversation, we discovered that we had a friend in common who worked for another insurance company. I have since contacted his friend and started a business correspondence with the Vice-president.

Small world? Certainly it is. What are the chances, first of either of these people being aboard the same two aircraft that I am on, and secondly of my sitting next to both of them? I would never have known if I had not decided to initiate a conversation.

Summary

1. A major factor in influencing others is how well you interact with them.
2. Social and business rapport is the lubricant which smooths the interface of all effective communication.
3. Look at things from three viewpoints: your point of view, the other person's point of view and by imagining how an outsider might see things.
4. Avoid the temptation to challenge values and deeply held beliefs. The art of influence is to encourage people to question their own viewpoints and to generate changes themselves.
5. By meeting others as frequently as possible you will consolidate the relationship you have formed and developed. This will help create opportunities to reinforce the need they have for you and your ideas and influence.
6. Most people only self-disclose because they want you to enquire into what they have said or indicated. All good social conversationalists strive to self-disclose in order to discover what they have in common. They look for similarities and strive to minimize the differences. So do the world's most successful salespeople.

Chapter 6

Understanding non-verbal communication

The meaning of your communication is the response it gets from other people. If you notice that the reaction is not the one you want, change what you are doing or saying until you achieve the appropriate response.

It's not what you say, it's the way that you say it. This chapter shows how and why body language supports or conflicts with the words you use, and how you can heighten your sensory acuity in order to interpret the body language of others and so gauge your success.

The 1960 televised presidential debate between Richard Nixon and John F. Kennedy says more about the impact of non-verbal communication or body language than any training film. Those who heard the debate on radio or who read transcripts in their newspaper felt that Nixon performed far better than Kennedy. People watching the debate live or on their TV felt differently. Their interpretation was enhanced and changed through seeing the body language signals which accompanied the words and voice tones.

Much has been written about the interpretation and use of body language in persuasive communication. I do not intend to cover body language in detail—it is sufficient to emphasize its importance and to highlight one or two points. There are many good books available on the subject, e.g. *Bodily Communication*, M. Argyle (Methuen & Co. Ltd, 1981); *Body Language*, Dr J. Braysich (Joseph Braysich & Associates, 1979); *Body Language*, Allan Pease (Sheldon Press, 1981).

In the last two decades research in British and American universities in particular has demonstrated that the non-verbal components of communication play a far more important role than was previously recognized. Further research has suggested that the non-verbal aspect outweighs the verbal in both accuracy and validity. Body language and voice tonality have an enormous influence on anyone listening to us. Unfortunately, there is little that we can do quickly to correct wrong impressions, once they have developed. We all know how difficult it is to rid ourselves of any old-established negative feelings we may harbour about another person. Communication is much more than the words we say.

Face-to-face verbal communication does not operate in a vacuum. The words and voice tones we choose are always accompanied by complementary body movements—posture and gestures. Subconscious and sublimated thoughts and feelings are openly expressed in the postures and gestures which accompany our words. People with good sensory acuity and empathy will pick up these unconscious signals and draw conclusions from them. Women seem particularly sensitive to these subliminal personal messages. Recent studies at Oxford University and in the USA have shown that women appear to be more aware of non-verbal communication signals than their male counterparts. (Victor Hugo once said that while men have foresight, women have insight.)

Being more aware of your non-verbal behaviour and that of others results in more effective influencing communication—both ways. For the purposes of acting 'as if', we need to remember one simple principle:

Meaningful interpretation of body language can only be made from gesture clusters.

A gesture cluster is a set of related movements—body posture, hands and arms, feet, head, as well as facial expression. Before embarking on your influencing communication consider how you want to be seen by the other person. Ask yourself a few questions about the way you want to appear:

- confident?
- relaxed?
- dynamic?
- controlled?
- enthusiastic?
- honest?

Exercise—Minimizing the guesswork

Imagine that you have an important meeting with a person who you wish to influence in some way. You have their undivided attention for half an hour.

1. What impressions of you would you like this person to take away with them when they leave?

2. How will you control and use your body posture in order to emphasize the way in which you want to be seen?

3. How will you control your gestures? What gestures would be seen as appropriate?

4. How and where will you sit or stand?

5. How will you control and use your facial expressions?

Using the appropriate tone of voice

A few years ago my son was confronted by his grandmother. Imagine the scene. Elderly figure of authority standing over small boy, wagging finger. There is a frown on her face, she looks as if she means business.

'You are a naughty little boy, aren't you?'
'Yes', said Sam, grinning up at her. She laughs and ruffles his hair.

What exactly is going on here? How could he misinterpret her reprimand? How did he get away with it? When we read grandma's words we can't hear the tone of voice she adopted. She had a laugh, a lilt in her voice. The end of the sentence lifted and indicated her approval and pleasure at her 'naughty' grandson. Communication is so much more than the words we speak. These form only a very small part of our expressiveness as human beings. For instance, research shows that when we meet someone for the first time only 7% of our initial impact on others is determined by the contents of what we say. The other 93% of our message is made up of body language (55%) and the tone of our voice (38%) (Figure 6.1).

Make sure that your body language and your tone of voice underpin the influencing message you want to convey.

Observing the reaction to our message

How often have you met a friend and been able to notice before either of you has said a word exactly how they are feeling? Perhaps you don't know why they feel that way, just that they do. 'It was written all over her face', 'If looks could kill' are familiar expressions and indicate the power of sensory awareness. Some people are better than others at gaining information this way. For some of us it represents a completely new channel of communication. Clearly, it can be dangerous to jump to conclusions. I have a friend who

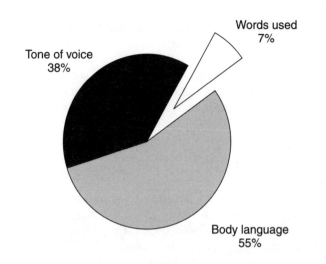

Figure 6.1 *Value placed against body language and voice tone*
Source: Mehrabian and Ferris, 1967, 'Inference of
Attitudes from Non-verbal Communication in Two
Channels', *The Journal of Counselling Psychology*, Vol. 31,
pp 248–252.

walks about with a permanent look of worry on his face.
When I first met him I noticed this and would often ask:
'Are you feeling all right? Is there anything I can do to
help?' He would usually respond with surprise, saying that
there was nothing wrong. After a while I began to realize
that this was the case—he just *looked* worried.

Notice how others respond to your influence, logging as
much data as you are able, then notice it a second and third
time. When you are confident that your assessments are
accurate you can proceed with more certainty. Heightening
your natural skills will help you predict with greater accuracy
how others might respond to your suggestions. As soon as
you are skilled at predicting the likely response you can
begin to choose the words which will achieve that response.

Whenever we communicate with other people we obtain
a reaction. Even if they say nothing and walk away from us,
that is a reaction. One of the influencer's most invaluable
skills is that of 'sensory awareness'—the ability to use all

our senses to read the reactions produced from our messages to others. (The so-called 'sixth' sense is simply when we are using the five senses but are unable to describe the way in which we sense information.) If we notice a positive reaction this will encourage us further. If the reaction is not what we want, we alter our approach until we achieve the desired reaction.

The eyes have it

We all know that when people are lying (or modifying the truth) they will avoid looking at us. Or, because they know this themselves, they will spend the whole time staring fixedly at our eyes saying: 'No, honestly . . . really . . . that's the truth'—and we still know they are lying.

When you are talking with a friend or colleague begin to notice what happens to the micro-muscles which cluster around their eyes. Notice how the 'bags' will puff up when they genuinely smile and laugh. How their eyes narrow when they are puzzling over what you just said. How their pupils dilate with pleasure or desire.

The mouth

Surrounded by numerous tiny muscles, the mouth is a positive goldmine of additional information providing invaluable clues to people's responses. Notice how people will contrive to hide their mouth whenever they are distorting the truth. They may do this in a whole-hearted fashion, covering their mouth with their entire hand. Or perhaps it is a subtle touch of the end of their nose with the top of their forefinger—so fast you'll miss it if you blink.

Watch how a mouth contracts or expands with passing emotions. In particular, observe the lower lip which most people find almost impossible to control when emotions course through the rest of their body. The lower lip is a great give-away, tightening perhaps with doubt or fear, expanding and filling out with delight, pleasure or surprise, trembling with sadness or remorse, and moistening with desire.

Flesh tone

Notice changes in flesh colour. Facial coloration often changes with stress. It may be the only outward sign that the other person is feeling stressed. Some people blush at the drop of a hat and this may signify nothing at all. It is possible to go white with fear, as the blood drains rapidly from the face. Watch for minute changes in skin colour. Look for patches or portions which change—the forehead may stay pale while cheeks, chin or even neck become redder in patches.

Changes in breathing rate

Have you ever given a speech or attended a difficult interview? Were you aware of the way these stressful circumstances affected your breathing? Probably it came higher up your chest, more shallow, faster. When you are relaxed breathing becomes calmer and slower, from the lower abdomen.

Two things you can be sure of: one—different people breathe in different ways at different moments; two—any noticeable shift in breathing will indicate a change in the way that person is thinking or feeling.

Exercise—Assessing non-verbal signals

1. Next time you are with someone who is familiar to you (partner, colleague, boss) make a series of proposals to them, e.g. 'Shall we go out tonight?', 'How about seeing a film?', 'Why don't we see the new Spielberg which is on at the Odeon?', anything reasonably within the normal scope of conversation with this individual.

Continued

2. Each time you make a suggestion notice their physical response.

3. Are the physical signals you notice congruent with the verbal responses?

4. What are those physical signals?
    - Eye movements
    - Lower lip changes
    - Skin colour changes
    - Changes in breathing

5. Now, using a different set of suggestions, run the exercise again with the same person.

6. How accurately are you able to predict their physical or verbal responses? How does this affect the ways in which you change your tactics?

7. To be certain that your calibrations are accurate, run the exercise at least one more time (each person's responses will be different, so you will need to run it separately for different individuals).

You are what you wear

Throughout the world clothing is used for modesty, comfort and display. It tells the society in which we live and work a lot about us. We make conscious daily decisions about the messages we want to give to other people through our garments. Just as voice tone, posture and gesture underscore our influencing messages, so too does the clothing we choose to wear. It can heavily influence the way in which we are seen by others and the way in which our messages are received.

Self-disclosure also takes place non-verbally. For example, the clothes you choose to wear are intended to make some sort of statement about yourself. A salesman attending one of my training seminars told an interesting story. It seems that whenever he left the office to sell he had with him three changes of clothing which he switched to match the person or organization to whom he was selling. How did he do this? (*Where* did he do it?) Outfit one was a grey suit; he would substitute the suit jacket for either a blazer (outfit two) or a leather jacket (outfit three). His job was to sell newspaper advertising to a wide variety of businesses—smart offices, advertising agencies, run-down back street car lots. By providing himself with several dress options he was expanding his opportunities to match the people to whom he sold.

But be careful, too much flexibility can work against you. Recently my wife and I were contacted by a company specializing in rendering the outside walls of houses and commercial buildings. They had perfected a system of coating a wall with a thick and impenetrable waterproof cement. Coincidentally we had been experiencing serious dampness in the front wall of the old house we live in so we were very open to any suggestions which might solve this problem. The company made an appointment for their surveyor to investigate, report back on his findings and recommend a solution.

That evening a van drew up outside the house and the surveyor knocked on the door. He was a middle-aged man, dressed in a dark grey boilersuit. He carried a metal case in one hand and introduced himself as the chief surveyor of the Such and Such Rendering Company. We let him in and talked for a while about the problems we had been experiencing. He listened carefully, made a few notes and asked if he could give the outer wall a thorough inspection. He left us looking at a video of his company's innovative rendering technique. As we dutifully watched the short film we could hear the surveyor outside, tapping away at the wall. When he had finished, he sat down and quietly and confidently talked us through his findings and the technicalities of his proposed solution. We were both impressed. He was serious, just technical enough for us and, of course, he was appropriately dressed. He left, saying that he would call back the next day and give us a written quotation.

The following evening promptly at seven o'clock he arrived. No grey boilersuit, no metal box, not even a van. He was driving a smart new red car, carried a bulging brief-case and wore an expensive-looking dark suit with a loud silk tie and very shiny shoes. His whole approach was different. As he turned on the charm, the sales talk and eventually the pressure it became very obvious that yesterday's 'surveyor' had become today's salesman. The quiet, serious man we had trusted twenty-four hours previously had disappeared. It was Doctor Jekyll and Mr Hyde all over again and we could not wait to be rid of Mr Hyde.

Think about what you will wear when you next attempt to influence others. Ask yourself these questions:

- What clothing is likely to be considered inappropriate by the other person?
- What clothing is the most appropriate for the circumstances and the message I need to convey?
- What clothing will the other person or people be wearing?
- To what extent do I need to conform to their style of clothing?
- Should I ignore them and simply wear what they would expect me to wear?

It is impossible to wear clothing without sending social signals. Every outfit tells a story.

Congruence

Have you ever noticed that sometimes spoken words do not appear to tally with the body language you are observing? Perhaps the other person is looking particularly relaxed, leaning back in a comfortable chair, uttering words like: 'This is *really* important. It is *essential* that we do something about it—right away!' Clearly, the speaker is just saying the words—words which do not seem to underline the urgency which they are stressing. They look far too relaxed to want to do anything much.

What you are noticing here is a lack of congruity. It is interesting that when there are confused messages being received, most people read the body language and do not believe the actual words spoken.

But beware. Lack of congruity can weaken your own messages. How often have you found yourself extolling the virtues of some idea just because your manager or partner told you to—not because you actually believed what you were asked to say? Chances are that your body language, your non-verbal signals, will give you away. As a general rule the more familiar you are with a person the more likely you are to be tuned in to their non-verbal signals. Have you ever wondered why it is that a dog will know well in advance that it is time for the evening walk? A standard pattern of behaviour has built up over time; the dog becomes aware of certain signals which always culminate in him being taken out. Rather like Pavlov's dogs, he begins to salivate before the event takes place. Anyone who lives, or works with, another person for any length of time begins to find that they are often one jump ahead of the other person's behaviour, thoughts and comments. For instance, I can always tell when my wife is worrying about something. She has a habit of cupping her chin in her hand. Even at some distance, my sensory acuity is sufficiently tuned in to my wife's characteristic body language patterns—as it should be, after 25 years of marriage.

Look for clusters of signals

One swallow doesn't make a summer and one body language signal does not necessarily make a message. Non-verbal communication is full of ambiguities. A simple shrug of the shoulder can mean many things: resignation—don't care—don't know. When someone tugs slowly at their ear lobe, does this mean that they are racked with self-doubt—or does their ear lobe itch?

When you are seated listening to someone a typical cluster of signals might consist of:

- leaning slightly forward in the chair
- hand/fingers grouped around chin
- head tilted slightly to the left
- a narrowing of the eyes
- good eye contact
- slow nods of the head.

This cluster of half a dozen separate signals could suggest that you are listening intently *(leaning forward/eye contact/ eyes narrowing)*, evaluating what they say *(fingers clustered around chin)*, agreeing with them or their points *(head tilted/ slow nods)*.

Changes in body language

Some people are often so wrapped up in what they are saying, so in love with their own voice that they fail to notice the changes in body language which are unfolding before them.

A colleague who started off looking alert, interested and keen slowly reveals that they are not so enthusiastic after all. The forward-leaning person with good eye contact gradually becomes slouched, fidgety and awkward, no longer giving good eye contact but taking furtive peeks at their watch. Worse still, it is possible to overlook the person who starts off appearing as if they are not in the least bit interested then slowly changes posture and gesture, suggesting that their level of interest has risen. Think about the number of people you know who simply miss these signals, even though they are taking place right under their noses.

Next time you need to influence others you may notice that your senses are more tuned in to what is going on around you. You may observe the other person's initial posture and register this in your memory, so that even small changes are easily noticed.

Summary

1. Body language, or non-verbal communication, is a language within a language and can go unnoticed.

2. The non-verbal contents of a communication outweigh the verbal in both accuracy and validity.

3. Don't ignore individual signals—but remember, a cluster of congruent signals sends a powerful message.

4. The meaning of your communication is the response that you elicit. If the reaction is not what we want we will need to change what we are saying or doing to get the appropriate response.

5. Non-verbal communication includes the clothing you choose to wear.

6. Are you giving out the signals you want to give out? Do they support your message? Your non-verbal communication supports and sustains your message. Be sure that it is the message you want to give. (But don't spend so much time concentrating on your own non-verbal signals that you forget about the other person.)

7. Our internal responses are reflected in our external behaviour.

8. Watch for changes in body language—from interest to lack of interest (or vice versa).

Chapter 7

Applying the power of personality

What you are sounds so loudly in my ears that I cannot hear what you say. R.W. Emerson

Conflicts of personality can create barriers to influencing success—your personality, and the personalities of others. This chapter helps you learn more about your personality and shows what can be done to utilize its strengths and ways in which you can minimize any weaknesses. It also details ways in which you can deal more effectively with those whose personality does not match your own.

Interacting with other people forms a large part of the social fabric of everyday life. Our ability to conform to social expectations is one of the factors taken into account whenever we try to influence others. As soon as we are old enough we are taught 'rules' by our parents and teachers. These appear to be designed to influence the way in which other people will react towards ourselves. From the very beginning, our earliest transactions with the rest of humanity illustrate just how anxious we are to convince everyone that we are socially competent and therefore somehow 'right' to be with. Some of these 'rules' could be:

- It is rude to stare at strangers.
- Do not speak before you are spoken to.
- Don't answer back.
- Respect your elders and betters.
- Do up your buttons, brush your hair.
- Children should be seen but not heard.

Conversation, whether business or social, is an intricate skill. Special verbal and interactive skills are needed if we are to make friends and influence people. If we fail to master conversational strategies and tactics across a wide range of relationships we inevitably weaken our power to influence others. Obviously it is easier to convince people with whom we have a good relationship or have something in common. The difficulty arises when we meet people who have personalities with which we find it difficult to relate.

Recently a colleague had to meet a new training manager, a man taking over the role from someone she had worked with for several years. She had formed a good working relationship with the old training manager. He was a rather dry and elderly gentleman with not much of a sense of humour but my colleague and he saw eye to eye and worked well together. The new man, who was about to take over, was very different. Apart from a keen sense of fun, he brought an intellectual mind to his work. He was younger and more creative and innovative. Despite two very different personalities my colleague managed to interact well with both men. She carefully nurtured both relationships. She did not pretend to be anyone other than herself but did take care which aspects of her personality were on show at any one time. With Dave, the younger man, she was a more creative-talker and fun to be with. They shared many laughs and bounced many workable creative ideas off one another. Meanwhile, she admired Mike the older man for his careful and dedicated approach to the job. He was slow and invariably took the traditional path but in his slightly ped-antic way managed to run an extremely efficient department.

One day Mike suggested that the three meet to discuss the year ahead. My colleague's heart sank. This would be the first time she had met both men together. The thought of being a pig in the middle of these two was daunting. It would mean that she would be forced to reveal aspects of her personality which she had spent time shielding both from. It was a difficult meeting which she sur-vived—but only just. The problem lay in the fact that the two relationships had flourished apart. If my colleague had worked with both men I expect her behaviour would have been more even, appealing to both their personalities.

This is perfectly normal. Anyone with a modicum of empathy will take care to adapt their behaviour to suit both circumstances and people. A couple of years ago in the space of two weeks my wife and I were invited to a funeral, a wedding in France and a christening. Needless to say we behaved quite differently on each occasion. We dressed differently, spoke in a different manner and tone, said dif-ferent things.

Exercise—How to be a chameleon

1. Think of a person with whom you have a good relationship. Someone in whose company you feel relaxed and comfortable.

   Describe how you behave towards them:

2. Now recall someone with whom you do not have a good relationship. Every time you see or hear this person your heart sinks. They make you feel and act in a different manner.

Continued

Describe how you typically behave towards this person:

3.   What are the main differences in your behaviour which make you a chameleon?

Much of our understanding of human behaviour stems from the work of Carl Jung (1875–1961). Jung found that there are recognized and repeated patterns in our behaviour. These patterns of habitual behaviour stem from our upbringing and development at home, in school and in society; they are developed early and are difficult, although not impossible, to change. Because we all possess our own set of preferred behaviours we can easily become attracted to certain types of people, organizations and interests. At the same time we may make decisions, often unconsciously, to reject some people and groups in society. These decisions frequently reflect our ingrained understanding of those personality characteristics which appear to mesh best with our own.

Jung's research identified four pairs of behaviour and found that most of us engage in only one of each pair with any success. He also found that almost all the people he analysed had developed one of these paired traits more than the other. Each trait is useful for certain tasks/jobs/professions but often creates problems with other tasks.

Carl Jung's four pairs of personality characteristics are:

More extrovert   or   More introvert

More extrovert: relates more easily to the outside world of people and things rather than ideas. More introvert: relates more easily to the inner world of ideas rather than the outer world of people and things.

Sensing   or   Intuiting

Sensing: preferring to work with known facts than look for possibilities in relationships. Intuiting: preferring to look for possibilities and relationships than work with known facts.

Thinking   or   Feeling

Thinking: basing judgements more on impersonal analysis and logic than on personal values. Feeling: basing judgements more on personal values than on impersonal analysis and logic.

Judging   or   Perceiving

Judging: liking a planned, decided, orderly way of life better than a flexible, spontaneous way. Perceiving: liking a flexible, spontaneous way of life better than a planned, decided, orderly way.

Since the publication of Carl Jung's *Psychological Types* (1921) much development has taken place in this field of human understanding. Most successful influencers seem to want to understand the mainsprings of their own behaviour and that of the people who they wish to influence. If personality is such an important factor in successful human interaction, today's influencer must understand elementary psychology if they are to improve rapport.

Here is a simple and accessible model, easy to understand and interpret. Try this questionnaire on yourself (or ask a colleague, friend or someone who knows you well to complete it on your behalf). It will tell you a great deal about the way in which you influence others as well as how you yourself might prefer to be influenced.

I Do it My Way—questionnaire

Everyone is uniquely different. Our faces are different, our bodies are different and we have differently 'shaped' personalities. There is no such thing as a right or wrong personality—people just think and act differently in different influencing situations.

I Do it My Way is an activity designed to help you to understand better how to influence others. The results will enable you to determine what kinds of personality you prefer to influence as well as those personalities which may be more difficult and less comfortable for you. Whatever your personality, it will provide you with many strengths, helping you to influence, persuade and convince others. It will inevitably also reveal some blind spots in your understanding of others and the way you respond to their personalities.

Directions

The following questionnaire consists of 20 pairs of statements. Read each statement and circle *one* statement in *each pair* which is most characteristic of you or your behaviour as you perceive it. Evaluate your behaviour as it is now, not as it once was or how you would like it to be.

1. **A** I enjoy making new friends
   B I would rather read than talk

2. **C** I find detail tedious and often unnecessary
   D I try to stick to the rules

3. **A** I love being with other people
   B I do not mind being on my own

4. **C** I tend to take charge
   D I am willing to be influenced by others

5. **A** I am comfortable talking to people I don't know
   B I am slow in developing new relationships

6. **C** I exert my influence on others
   D I am easy to persuade

7. **A** I enjoy social gatherings
   B I am just as happy to be on my own

8. **C** I am confident of my views and opinions
   D I am happy for others to take charge

9. **A** I have been accused of being 'loud'
   B I keep to a small circle of friends

10. **C** I express my beliefs with confidence
    D I sometimes keep quiet even when I know I am right

11. **A** I dislike too much detail
    B I am very thorough and careful

12. **C** I can plan and control the work of others
    D I am uncertain of my views

13. **A** I tend to be rather impulsive
    B I look before I leap

14. **C** I have clear aims and ambitions
    D I live each day as it comes

15. **A** I am an approachable person
    B I keep myself to myself

16. **C** I am a poor delegator
    D I seek the approval of others

17. **A** I make new friends easily
    B I am happy with my own company

18. **C** I achieve, others can look after the detail
    D I am willing to be influenced by others

19. **A** I am a people person
    B I take time to form relationships with others

20. **C** I take the lead in group work
    D I am easily influenced

Scoring and interpretation

1. Count the number of As and Bs you circled and record the number in the spaces below. Likewise, total the Cs and Ds.
2. Subtract the number of As from the number of Bs and the Cs from the Ds.
    The differences can range from +10 to –10.
    Transfer the differences to the scoring profile.

    .... (B) minus .... (A) = ...
    .... (D) minus .... (C) = ...

Scoring profile

Extrovert　　　　　　**(B minus A)**　　　　　　　**Introvert**
–10 –9 –8 –7 –6 –5 –4 –3 –2 –1 0 +1 +2 +3 +4 +5 +6 +7 +8 +9 +10

Dominant　　　　　　**(D minus C)**　　　　　　　**Submissive**
–10 –9 –8 –7 –6 –5 –4 –3 –2 –1 0 +1 +2 +3 +4 +5 +6 +7 +8 +9 +10

Transferring and reading your score

To obtain a graphic representation (Figure 7.1) of the relative importance of each score to your overall behaviour, plot your Extrovert/Introvert score (horizontal axis) against your Dominant/Submissive score (vertical axis). Now plot the co-ordinates represented by each mark on the axes. Your final score will reveal you to be one of four personality types:

- Dominant/Extrovert (proactive-leader)
- Dominant/Introvert (creative-talker)
- Submissive/Extrovert (analytical-listener)
- Submissive/Introvert (reactive-follower)

Respondents whose scores are closest to one of the four

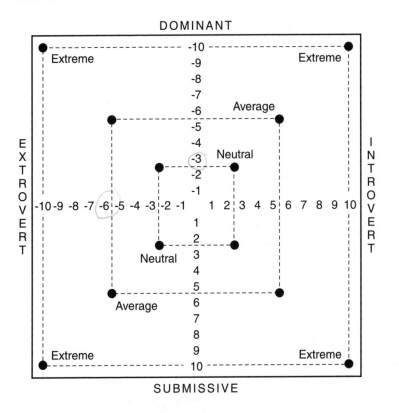

Figure 7.1 *Scoring chart*

outer corners of the main box are extreme examples. Respondents whose scores fall on or within the central zone are average examples and respondents whose scores are closest to zero are neutral examples.

Although this model is simple when compared with Jung's findings, most of his key personality characteristics can be overlaid on it. By recognizing and interpreting the effect of these characteristics you can adjust more easily to another's personality.

To engage more successfully with a wide range of individuals and stand a better chance of influencing change you need to be prepared to amplify (or suppress) the appropriate characteristics in your own personality. To guide you through this model I have created a matrix, with each of the four 'types' given a name. It will help you to identify the personalities of those people who you need to influence. As a by-product you may begin to realize exactly why it is that you form better relationships with some than others.

Developed as a matrix, the personality model looks like this:

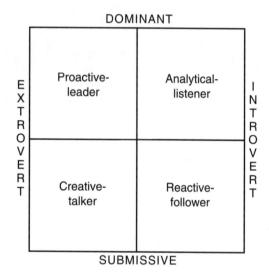

Figure 7.2   *Personality types*

I use this model frequently in sales training seminars presented around the world. A question I usually ask the people present is: 'To which of the four personality types do you least like presenting your case?' The results are fascinating. There are often one or two people who dislike analytical-listener and reactive-follower.

This is an interesting phenomenon. It is perfectly understandable that salespeople may feel uneasy in the company of either of these two types. After all, neither analytical-listener nor reactive-follower has much in common with the average salesperson, who is often an extrovert (whether dominant or submissive). Experience suggests that although analytical-listener and reactive-follower may be slow in coming to a final decision they usually become loyal, solid customers who will be slow to change to another supplier.

Research shows that two personality traits attract one another:

- Those who look after or lead (someone who is dominating) are attracted to those who want to be looked after or guided (someone who is submissive) and vice versa. This phenomenon is known as nurturing and succouring.
- Some dominating people are the bullying boss (or husband or wife!) who feels better when surrounded by sycophantic, subservient slaves. Nurturing/succouring does not enter these relationships.

If you are more submissive than dominant, this is not to say that you should change your personality. Just modify certain aspects—if necessary—when in the company of more dominant types. If you are influencing or persuading someone who is dominating it would be unwise to show yourself as being too submissive. If you doubt this, ask yourself 'Who does a dominating person play golf with at the weekend?' A bunch of submissive people? Of course not. Most true dominant types revel in the company of other dominant people. To build a relationship with a dominant personality, bring out your own dominant characteristics and use your rapport and matching skills. In short, if you feel that a 'personality conflict' is interfering with your relationship it is important to notice early on in the relationship whether the other person has a role which they prefer playing and to make the necessary adjustments—if you don't adjust, it is unlikely that the person who you are attempting to convince will alter.

Personality model analysed

To help identify and understand the four 'types' we now present a detailed analysis of the personality matrix. Each personality type has both positive and negative features which can help or hinder your efforts. These are analysed below.

Proactive-leader: wants to be in charge all the time

For many people, influencing proactive-leaders is an uphill struggle. Proactive people initiate and frequently jump into situations without much thought or analysis. They often upset people because they bulldoze their ideas through all argument. This character wants to dominate every conversation he or she is involved in. Most people find this quite intimidating. Every time you manage to gain entry to the conversation and start to make a suggestion or two, the pro-active-leader ignores you or hi-jacks your ideas and claims them as his/her own. Here lies the main route to convincing a proactive-leader—let them think that your ideas are theirs. Do not worry unnecessarily that it is your idea. The point is that the proactive-leader thinks it is theirs. Let him/her— after all your main objective is to gain commitment—and you have that. They are good at getting the job done, so let them go ahead—even if it is your idea.

Another way through the bluster and bluff is to engage in the fight. The proactive-leader despises very submissive behaviour. He/she cannot engage in a one-sided fight. He/she relishes a battle and likes to feel that they have 'won' a victory.

Often a self-made person (and proud of it), this character can appear coarse and materialistic. He/she is egotistical and conscious of status (measured by anything from age to height, job title to wealth, size of car to member-ship of exclusive clubs). All possible arguments should be expressed in ways that boost his or her prestige. Don't worry too much about flattery. The proactive-leader expects to be flattered—it is all part of his/her motivation. Use power words like:

- Best
- Biggest
- Unique to you
- Powerful
- First
- Ahead of the pack
- Money

If this seems unsubtle—it is! But subtlety is not his/her style. Ask his/her opinion, allow him/her to be magnanimous. The proactive-leader can be kind as well as a bully.

Positive and negative characteristics

+ Planner; goal setter; disciplined; organized; open to new ideas; enjoys open power; appears confident; authoritative; makes statements; task oriented; makes quick decisions; can be kind and helpful.
− Insensitive; easily bored; bullies people; aggressive; overbearing; impatient; direct; ruthless; a poor delegator.

Analytical-listener: wants to feel in charge

Like the proactive-leader, the analytical-listener is dominant. He or she can be aloof and quiet. This type prefers you to do all the talking, hoping perhaps that you will talk your way out of your own argument or, even better, make mistakes and reveal the weaknesses of your case. This one is very objective, focused and, above all, cool. Carefully framed questions will bring him or her out of their shell. Use their ideas and opinions to support your case.

Power words and phrases which will help your argument include:

- Statistical proof
- Evidence
- Facts and figures

- Research
- Profit
- Logical
- Reason

Like the proactive-leader, the analytical-listener is strongly independent. He/she genuinely wants to think things over. This need should not necessarily be seen as a rejection. The analytical-listener did not achieve his/her current position by making hasty decisions. He/she wants to assess all the data. Be prepared to put your case in writing for the analytical-listener. He/she will want to go over the arguments in his/her own time. Provide plenty of charts, graphs and tables. The analytical-listener will love poring over them. But make quite sure they are accurate. This type searches for inaccuracies and derives fiendish pleasure in discovering a few.

Positive and negative characteristics

+ Thorough; persistent; calm; relishes hidden power; formal; disciplined; active; thoughtful; subtle; deliberate; objective; rational; analytical; logical; loves figures.
− Perfectionism slows down decisions; aloof; procrastinates; closed to new ideas; hates open persuasion; outwardly unemotional; cruel sense of humour; distant; slow to trust; bureaucratic; demands evidence.

Reactive-follower: seeks a dependent relationship

Like the analytical-listener this type is also a reserved person. Reactive people wait for others to take the initiative and then follow. They have a need to consider and analyse before acting. They spend much time waiting as they study situations endlessly. He or she is timid and uncertain, relying heavily on advice and counsel from a wide variety of sources. The reactive-follower has a long record of bad decisions. Because of this he or she rarely attains a position of authority, especially one where contacts with the outside world involve purchasing or making major decisions. However, there are many managers and owners of small businesses who epitomize the classic reactive-follower type. When this is the case their position is frequently reached by default or inheritance. The reactive-follower is a most loyal employee and should on no account be pushed or manipulated.

Power words which work particularly well include:

- Security
- Safety
- Guaranteed
- Reliability
- Popular
- Tried and tested
- Fail safe
- Proven

As decisions can take considerable time it is important to maintain the relationship. Do not leave the reactive-follower on his/her own. Keep by his/her side, helping, showing, supporting, proving. You will almost certainly have to expend considerable support effort which can become frustrating. But if this means that you are eventually seen by the reactive-follower as someone to trust and rely on, then all that time and effort you spent will turn out to be a worthwhile investment.

Positive and negative characteristics

+ Good listener; dependable; friendly; passive; gentle; quiet; thoughtful; informal; loyal; people oriented.
− Cautious; easily acquiesces; submissive; slow to trust; requires proof; relies on advisers; hates detail; dislikes change.

Creative-talker: wants a social relationship

More salespeople have fallen foul of this type than perhaps any other. The problem is simple. At first glance the creative-talker is such a sociable and friendly type, so helpful and supportive, making everything seem easy. This is often an illusion. The creative-talker's chief concern is to make people like him/her. He/she is above all a people person, and keen to maintain the relationship. His/her approach to business can be sloppy and disorganized. He/she makes and breaks promises, misses appointments, keeps you waiting.

The key to a successful dialogue with the creative-talker is control. Control the conversation: 'I have come to see you today, Mr Creative-talker, to discuss the MacCallum project.' This statement anchors your objective at the outset. Every time the creative-talker changes the subject you can turn it back on track by 'going back to the reason for our meeting'.

Power words which work well with this type include:

- Fun
- Appreciate
- Enjoy
- Convenient
- Easy
- Trouble free
- Inexpensive

The creative-talker type can be fun to be with but beware— he or she is sometimes so anxious to preserve the friendship, or business relationship, that solutions may never be found or decisions agreed.

Positive and negative characteristics

+ Responsive; talkative; very sociable; friendly; informal; warm; approachable; creative; relishes new ideas; enthusiastic.
- Undisciplined; poor time-keeper; disorganized; impul-

sive; gullible; easily led; impatient; over-generalizes; gets emotional and nostalgic.

Summary

1. Everyone is different. There is no such thing as a right or a wrong personality. People just think and act differently in different influencing situations.
2. Whatever your personality it will work for you and against you as it will always be interdependent on the personality of others.
3. Understanding your personality can help you to decide on a variety of strategic approaches with others.
4. Different approaches and different use of words and behaviour may be required depending on the strength of other people's personality.
5. Do not expect others to shift their personality to suit yours. Any changes must come from you if you are to succeed in influencing a greater variety of personalities.

Chapter 8

Choosing the right approach

One judges everyone by one's own standard and from one's own standpoint. M. Esther Harding

Different influencers achieve different results. This chapter outlines the benefits of a flexible approach to influence. Eight separate influencing styles are identified and a questionnaire helps you to understand your preferences.

I have a good friend, Jenny. Jenny was born in February which makes her an Aquarian. Whether you believe in astrology or not she typifies the sign of the water carrier. She has a great need for freedom and is strong-willed with firm convictions. She is slightly detached and unpredictable. She will not be pushed, bullied or browbeaten. If anyone tries to make her do anything against her will or better judgement they will find that their pressure has the reverse effect. Once she has dug her heels in they won't easily be prised out. The autocratic approach is doomed to failure. A careful argument backed up with proof and statistical evidence is challenged, queried and wrestled to death before any grudging acceptance is granted. A wholly passive approach is equally fruitless and frustrating. 'Well, come on,' she'll say, 'what do you think? If you don't know the answer you can't expect me to know what it is.' Probably a 'democratically assertive negotiation' is the only possible route to success with Jenny!

Another friend, William, is quite the reverse. He can never make up his mind. Give him two or more choices and you can wait for ever for a decision. If you try the democratic approach this only offers him even greater scope for vacillation (something his friends suspect that William rather enjoys). A passive response will lead eventually to a total communication vacuum. A good deal of the time William actually likes to be told what to do. If others are doing it too, then he is even more convinced (he would hate to be a guinea pig for some half-baked idea which has not been thoroughly tested). He wants proof and supportive evidence to shore up his eventual decision. One of William's greatest fears is being held up to ridicule after he has made what he thinks is a carefully considered choice. 'Oh no, William, you didn't fall for that old scam, surely? They must have seen you coming a mile off.'

Two individuals who respond quite differently to influence. Behaviour which one finds unacceptable is highly productive with the other. Knowing the person you are influencing should be a prerequisite for eventual success. But what if you have never met them before? Recently I was introduced to someone who worked in a senior position with a management consultancy firm. She told me that her organization was expanding and becoming increasingly involved in a wider range of consultancy assignments. I found out some details from her: the type of work carried out by the consultants, the market sectors on which they concentrated and so on. I asked her to let me have a copy of the company brochure with the name of the managing director.

My objective was to persuade the organization to take me on their books or add my details to their database as a prospective consultant for future assignments. I wrote to the senior partner outlining my background and detailed a few current clients who in some way aligned with their own field of operation. By return I received a letter inviting me to meet with the Consultancy Director. OK so far, the first hurdle successfully jumped. The only problem was that I had never met the director in question. What was his background? What type of personality did he have? How old was he? How did he dress?

I asked my friend, the original contact, all these questions and more. Gradually I built up a clear picture of the person I was to meet. First I carefully reviewed my own work experience looking for anything which might dovetail with his own. On the morning of the meeting I considered what I would wear taking care to choose a shirt and tie which would signal that I was on the same level as he was, or at least not significantly different. Knowing a little more about his personality I was able to adopt the right frame of mind from the very start of the meeting. When we finally met one another the care and thought which I had invested paid off. There was still the need to become acquainted with one another at the start; still the need to go over my letter and curriculum vitae, but the pre-planning seemed to accelerate these formalities. Everything went faster and smoother than it often does when we meet someone for the first time.

Influencing behaviour is multi-faceted. From one communication to another we need to practise behavioural flexibility providing ourselves with the maximum opportunity for success. Each of us will be naturally and instinctively better able to deal with certain situations than others. Our strengths see us through. The only way to successfully influence change in different people and personalities is to learn and develop the widest possible range of influencing styles. Knowing your preferred styles will create a good foundation for further personal development and growth.

The following questionnaire has been designed to reveal your strengths and weaknesses as well as your preferred influencing styles.

Discovering your preferred influencing styles

What style will you choose?

Depending on what outcome you want, how much commitment you seek, how important the ongoing relationship is—
you will need to choose the style most suitable and follow
it through. If this fails it will be helpful to understand what
further styles may be available to you as this activity helps
you to develop an awareness of your preferred influencing
styles.

Directions

The following questionnaire consists of 32 pairs of statements. Circle *one* statement in *each pair* which best describes
your behaviour in most situations, most of the time.

1. **A**   I don't give up when others disagree
   B   I develop other people's ideas

2. **C**   I produce evidence to support my arguments
   D   I feel strongly about the outcome

3. **E**   I make my views clear
   F   I often regret not coming forward earlier

4. **G**   I explain the benefits of my proposals
   H   I try to seek a satisfactory compromise

5. **A**   I tell people exactly what I want
   B   I seek facts and opinions

6. **C**   I explain the facts
   D   I use my enthusiasm to convince

7. **E**   I am happy to fight my own corner
   F   I keep my feelings to myself

8. **G**   I enjoy convincing other people
   H   I seek a win/win solution

9. **A**   I put forward new ideas

	B	I am a good listener
10.	**C**	I provide statistical backup where necessary
	D	I can become upset if I fail to convince
11.	**E**	I express my beliefs with confidence
	F	I am afraid to admit my ignorance
12.	**G**	I plan answers to likely objections
	H	I trade concessions—give and take
13.	**A**	I contribute many suggestions
	B	I build on other people's ideas
14.	**C**	I construct a good logical argument
	D	I feel it personally if I fail to influence
15.	**E**	I tell people clearly how I feel
	F	I feel uncomfortable with compliments
16.	**G**	I push for an early decision
	H	I enjoy bargaining with others
17.	**A**	I am comfortable challenging the views of others
	B	I am willing to be influenced by others
18.	**C**	I put my case in writing
	D	I sweep people up with my enthusiasm
19.	**E**	I believe I have the right to say 'No'
	F	I feel uncomfortable in unfamiliar surroundings
20.	**G**	I can quickly think up a counter-argument
	H	I see the point of view of both sides
21.	**A**	I enjoy giving information
	B	I accept criticism without becoming defensive
22.	**C**	I provide step-by-step details
	D	I skip detail and influence through my personality
23.	**E**	I express my displeasure when appropriate
	F	I do favours when I prefer not to
24.	**G**	I enjoy persuading people to change their minds
	H	I am concerned about maintaining the relationship
25.	**A**	I feel comfortable giving orders

B   I listen carefully to people who disagree with me

26.   **C**   I present my ideas in an organized way
    D   I am elated when I succeed in influencing

27.   **E**   I don't mind asking for help when necessary
    F   I don't like hurting others' feelings

28.   **G**   I learn all the features and benefits of my proposals
    H   I try to understand the viewpoint of the other person

29.   **A**   I explain carefully my requirements
    B   I am happy to support other people's ideas

30.   **C**   I use facts to convince others
    D   My enthusiasm is contagious

31.   **E**   I express my feelings honestly and directly
    F   I try to maintain popularity with others

32.   **G**   I am not discouraged when others object
    H   I avoid conflict and seek a happy medium

Scoring

1.   Count the number of As and Bs you circled and record the number in the spaces below.
Likewise, total the Cs and Ds, the Es and Fs, the Gs and Hs.

2.   Subtract the number of As from the number of Bs, the Cs from the Ds, the Es from the Fs and the Gs from the Hs. The differences can range from +8 to −8. Transfer the differences to the scoring profile.

.... (B)   minus   .... (A)   = ...
.... (D)   minus   .... (C)   = ...
.... (F)   minus   .... (E)   = ...
.... (H)   minus   .... (G)   = ...

Scoring profile

A = Directive/push style   **B = Collaborative/pull style**
−8 −7 −6 −5 −4 −3 −2 −1   0 +1 +2 +3 +4 +5 +6 +7 +8

C = Logical style   **D = Emotional style**
−8 −7 −6 −5 −4 −3 −2 −1   0 +1 +2 +3 +4 +5 +6 +7 +8

E = Assertive style   **F = Passive style**
−8 −7 −6 −5 −4 −3 −2 −1   0 +1 +2 +3 +4 +5 +6 +7 +8

G = Persuasive style   **H = Bargaining style**
−8 −7 −6 −5 −4 −3 −2 −1   0 +1 +2 +3 +4 +5 +6 +7 +8

Interpretation

1. Extreme scores—minus 6, 7 or 8, plus 6, 7 or 8

If you scored at this level you probably tend to use that style rather than its paired opposite (e.g. assertive rather than passive). This could be because:

- you work in an organization or group where this style is the cultural norm;
- you work for, or closely with, an individual who expects you to use this style (possibly they use it a lot);
- you work in a job or function where this style is recognized as appropriate;
- none of the above applies—you simply prefer to behave that way.

2. Balanced scores—minus 2 or 1, zero; plus 1 or 2

If any of your scores fell within this range it suggests that you are equally able and prepared to use both paired styles (e.g. directive or collaborative). This provides you with greater flexibility of operation across a wider spectrum of influencing scenarios.

Question: What do the scores suggest to you about your preferred style of influencing?

Question: What are the likely gains and losses if you continue to use your preferred style? Are these the gains you seek?

Question: If you want a different outcome, which of your preferred styles will you need to change in some way?

Which influencing style will work best?

There are normally three objectives to be kept in mind whenever you influence others:

- you want to maintain an existing relationship;
- you aim to gain long-term commitment to your proposal;
- you wish to ensure that your message is passed on to other people.

All influence produces some sort of reaction. On a scale of one to five these are the most likely reactions you will receive:

1. Total commitment: 'Brilliant idea. Can't wait to start.'
2. Broad agreement: 'Like the idea but I have one or two questions.'
3. Compliance: 'OK. If that's what you want. You're the boss.'
4. Disagreement: 'There are three good reasons why this won't work.'
5. Sabotage: 'I may have agreed but I'm still not going to do it.'

Exercise—Gaining commitment

1. Recall a situation where you successfully managed to gain commitment from another person, or people.

2. As you think back to that time when you were successful begin to remember what it was you said or did which resulted in the commitment you sought.

3. What signals told you that the other person/people were committed?
   What did you hear?

   What did you see?

   What did you feel?

4. Will you want to repeat your success or alter your approach?

5. Now contrast this with a less successful occasion.

The eight styles of influence

1. The directive/push style

Autocracy generally works best when it is accompanied and supported by power, authority or status. You are the captain of the ship and you must be obeyed. The benefits this brings to the influencing process are few but very significant. First, autocracy is a fast and efficient way of persuasion. It is unlikely that there will be any serious objections to be overcome. The process will probably take the form of a monologue not a dialogue. You will issue commands and they will encounter little or no resistance.

A fast and efficient directive approach does have its downside. Because it is a one-way road for the people on the receiving end they have little opportunity to contribute to your proposal. It is presented as a *fait accompli* with full commitment expected. This expectation frequently backfires especially when long-term commitment is required. The problem often stems from the other person feeling 'You won and I lost'. Effective for short-term influencing—when you gain commitment be prepared to check and double-check that your proposals are being carried out as agreed. Only use your autocratic power when a short-term change is required. Do not be surprised if commitment is weak. Be prepared to enforce the commitment.

2. The collaborative/pull style

The joy of the more democratic approach is that it works successfully without being backed up by power. You don't need to be in charge or have any formal authority or status over others. Because you have included them in the decision process your ideas receive high commitment. Collaborative influence over others is therefore low risk and usually needs little enforcement as it is seen as 'you win/I win'. Because others contribute to and support your proposition this style of influence is most effective for long-term influencing. You will not need to enforce the agreement—too much 'policing' by you could even result in a withdrawal of support. If you do feel the need to follow up be sure to do it elegantly and discreetly and with empathy.

Democratic influencing is slow and not without some risks. True democracy means handing over the entire decision process to others. They may take their time and even resent it if you chivvy and chase them for a resolution. Who is to say that they will arrive at the 'answer' you seek? Suppose it is radically different and largely unworkable? They are now committed so will not be happy if you decide to change the requirements at this stage.

It is likely that you will want to think things through carefully before handing over the decision to others. Questions you may want to address could include:

- How long can I afford to wait for a decision?
- How many people can I usefully delegate this to?
- Who should I delegate it to?

What parameters should they work within? The more democratic choices you can offer the more commitment you will receive. The fewer parameters and conditions applied to the democratic process the better. Democracy takes time—be sure to give it time.

3. The logical style

Many people favour a logical explanation before reaching a decision. They may demand a blow-by-blow account of the background details, how you reached your conclusions, how many conclusions you examined, why you chose your particular recommended solution. For many of us this relentless concentration on detail can be tiresome and may dampen our enthusiasm. After all we are anxious to get on with the matters in hand. After a while we feel that it may be better to not bother at all.

The logical approach to influence can have very positive rewards. First it makes us examine and re-examine our arguments. No amount of enthusiasm will make someone agree to our suggestions if they have a detailed logical linear mind. The creative, spontaneous approach is not acceptable to this type. The only way we can be certain of a sympathetic ear to our argument is to do our homework. Leave nothing to chance—no guesswork, no exaggeration—just straightforward unassailable facts. And the more of them the better.

4. The emotional style

Appealing to the various emotions which swirl around within the human heart and mind can be dangerous. When emotions are captured by dubious arguments the result can be long-held feelings of remorse and anger. No-one likes to be duped, especially when it is later revealed that decisions were based on emotions rather than logic or good sense. Emotional decisions are frequently made on impulse. Perhaps feelings of sorrow or anger, love or hatred may allow us to be pushed into a hasty decision. And we have all encountered so-called emotional blackmail at some time in our lives. So whenever you attempt to harness other people's emotions take care to examine the likely outcome. If you desire a long-term commitment with no bad aftertaste or unnecessary remorse, appealing to emotions can be a very effective way of influencing. The submissive extrovert can be particularly susceptible to an emotional appeal.

Having checked the integrity of your objectives and motives it is quite in order to utilize charm and enthusiasm. Persuading others to feel part of your exciting project or idea is an extension of your own feelings. Enthusiasm has been defined as 'knowledge on fire'. Use your knowledge and enthusiasm to fire up the imaginations of others. This approach works well with those who are themselves emotional or impulsive. If they become swept up in the excitement of a project they are also likely to be captured by the charm, charisma or sheer enthusiasm of the influencer. By appealing to the long-term effects of your ideas you will also be stressing the continuing value they will gain from your ideas.

Some power words which work well could include:

- Pleasure
- Happiness
- Love
- Security
- Admiration
- Appreciation
- Satisfaction

Appealing to the emotions carries with it a risk. Check your motives carefully and remember that although this approach can be successful it can also leave a nasty taste in the mouth of those you persuade. Painful memories linger long—they'll get you next time!

5. The assertive style

Assertiveness is the use of clear and unambiguous language. By expressing your feelings you ask directly and confidently for what you want (or do not want). Being assertive does not involve aggression, simply firmness.

Maintain good eye contact, speak in a level and pleasant tone and express your needs unequivocally and concisely.

Making a request: 'Will you complete the report by Friday afternoon, please?'

Refusing a request: 'I'm sorry but I won't be able to give you a hand today. I have too much on at the moment.'

Coupled with assertiveness, persistence can work wonders. This is a technique known as 'broken record'. You make your statement and, depending on the response you get, you repeat it in a slightly different form. You do this as many times as is necessary for the other person to fully understand your intent.

Example: 'Can you word process this by 12 o'clock, please?'

'I appreciate what you say but this document must be ready for this afternoon's board meeting.'

'Your other work will have to be delayed in that case.'

'That is not good enough. I'll leave it with you and call back in an hour to see how you are progressing.'

Assertive influence works with autocratic people and those who least expect assertion from you. You believe in yourself, you act and initiate, rather than react.

6. The passive style

At first glance this seems an improbable notion. How can a person be passive or submissive and yet influence others and control the outcome? The passive approach suggests that the rights and needs of others take precedence over yours. If not controlled properly this can result in feelings of low self-esteem, frustration and even withdrawal.

Suppose that another driver cuts you up and after you shake your fist at him he stops and approaches your car. What do you do now? He is bigger, younger and fitter than you. Any argument could well lead to a physical encounter. You decide to make a joke of it. This means that you have to swallow your pride and back off. Some might say that this was wimpish behaviour. Others would agree that you took the sensible view and avoided further problems while you still had the time.

Remember the 80-year-old widow mentioned in Chapter 1? Her passive and submissive approach certainly had an influence on the robbers who raided her home. The option of influencing outcomes through submission is certainly viable as long as you can come to terms with any feelings it might create within you after the event. Don't dismiss the possibility of using passive or submissive behaviour. There may be many incidents in your life in which submission can pay dividends. The cost to you may be the question 'Can I live with my conscience?' as the passive approach can bring with it feelings of remorse and even self-loathing.

7. The persuasive style

Most people leave the scene when they see a salesperson on the horizon. We all have tales to tell of the archetypal pushy salesperson who pins you up against a wall and tries to thrust some product or service down your throat. Never mind whether you actually want it or not—the one they're selling is cheaper, faster, bigger and you would be a fool not to take advantage of their unique offer. Then there's the cold call. Just when you are sitting back in your chair for the first time all day the telephone or door bell rings—and it's your friendly salesperson reading out boring product details from a script.

There is often a case for good old-fashioned salesmanship.

Many people actually like to be sold to. Stroll through any street market anywhere in the world and you'll see crowds of happy punters being influenced by sales spiel. Recently my wife was cold-called by a salesman selling a carpet cleaning product. She agreed to see him and after an hour in his company was flicking through her telephone book happily providing him with names and numbers of all her closest friends. She was so taken with his sheer salesmanship and youthful exuberance that it seemed almost churlish not to oblige when he asked her to 'help him reach his sales targets' by giving him some referred leads. She truly appreciated his skill.

Although most of us do not like the sales type we are after all perpetual buyers. Hardly a day goes by when we aren't in and out of shops, or on the telephone checking comparative prices. In a typical year we might make purchasing decisions to buy a car or a holiday or even a job. And in most cases we will expect some sort of sales technique to come into play. We are buyers—and buyers need salespeople.

The straightforward 'sales' approach works well with anyone who expects to be sold to. A carefully planned sales case clearly shows how benefits match needs, objections can be overcome and aiming for a clear decision makes all the sense in the world. The influencing style, sometimes known as 'bridging', is an approach which works well with people who cannot stand the overt persuasive technique. There are three main paths to successful bridging. The first is to draw out the other person's point of view through careful questioning. Check their values and beliefs. Next demonstrate through rapport skills that you understand their point of view. Empathize without necessarily sympathizing. Finally lead them towards agreement by giving credit and praise in response to their good ideas and suggestions. Join your views with theirs and avoid disagreement. Demonstrate, whenever you can, exactly how your proposals dovetail with their own ideas and feelings. Sales techniques work best with those who buy. The extrovert personality is often more accepting of the overt sales approach. Make sure you have a watertight case if 'selling' your ideas to a dominant or submissive introvert.

8. The bargaining style

For many people there is little to distinguish bargaining from negotiating, or negotiating from selling. Frequently the sale will end in a bargaining session and the edges become blurred. The art of bargaining is as old as mankind's own history. Adam Smith, an eighteenth-century economist, suggested: 'Man is an animal that makes bargains. No other animal does this—no dog exchanges bones with another.' When salesperson meets potential buyer for the first time there is an imbalance. The salesperson's desire to sell something exceeds the buyer's desire to purchase. But it may be possible to add value through creative negotiation. Not just sharing the cake but making the cake bigger. When we decide to bargain our need to buy more or less equals the other person's need to sell. Proposals and counter-proposals lead eventually to an agreeable solution. Given common needs it will be the greater skill of the negotiator which leads to an acceptable win/win resolution.

The one question which should be at the forefront for anyone about to embark on bargaining for results is this:

To what extent do I need to maintain this relationship?

If the answer is 'very little' then it may not be necessary to conduct a fair negotiation. (This does not imply the use of underhand tactics, lying or cheating. The lack of an ongoing relationship between buyer and seller could result in either side agreeing to a solution which is ultimately found to be lacking in fairness. This will matter less if neither side find themselves facing each other across a negotiating table.) Good negotiators realize the importance of the ongoing relationship and work hard to seek a win/win resolution. Flexibility allows them to trade concessions for concessions. Very little is given away. Not surprisingly negotiation works well with anyone who expects to negotiate the final outcome. Here are a few basic rules:

1. Set your sights high. You will inevitably have to lower them during your negotiation so it makes sense to aim high. But not so high that it makes a negotiated outcome appear impossible.
2. Find out what people want before you begin the negotiation. They are bound to have a package of needs and unless you list these carefully before starting the dialogue there is every chance that they will spend the whole negotiation producing one demand after another. Then when you have run out of concessions to trade you will be forced to concede to their remaining demands in order to reach a final solution.
3. Don't give anything away. Always trade concessions. Give something away that they want, win something back that you want. Even the most unlikely elements can be traded for one another (time concessions for cost reductions; agreeing to leave the house you are selling earlier than you would like so as to be able to take the hall light fitting with you; asking for a better-grade car in return for a lower salary increase). Take care in evaluating the worth of a concession. It is easy to say yes to a request because the concession holds little value for you. Ask yourself: 'This is of little value to me—but how much is it worth to the other person?'
4. Be flexible. Continue to seek even the most improbable way out of any impasse. Both sides want to negotiate a solution so there should not be any need for the discussion to founder on apparently insoluble sticking points.

Exercise

1. Consider a forthcoming influencing situation. Work out your objectives and get them clear in your mind.
2. Think carefully about the person you plan to influence. Run through their likely values and beliefs. What is important to them? What are their thoughts? Think

---

Continued

about possible objections they may have to your
proposition.

3.   Choose two of the above influencing styles. Try
conflicting styles: autocratic or negotiation; selling or
bridging, for instance.

4.   Now brief a friend or colleague to role play these
situations with you. Explain that you are going to run
through the same situation but will be using two differing
styles of influence.

5.   Run the two role plays consecutively and without any
comment or discussion.

6.   Evaluate both role plays. Notice how you (and your
friend) felt as the role plays unfolded. Discuss the
changes in perception which took place during the role
plays.

7.   Consider how you will use these insights in the future
when you next want to influence others.

Summary

1.   Different people and different circumstances demand
flexibility of influencing style.

2.   Depending on your outcome you will need to choose
the style most suitable and follow it through.

3.   Only change style when you begin to notice that you
are unlikely to achieve your outcome if you continue.

4.   The influencer who possesses the widest range or choice
of style has the most flexibility of operation.

5.   The person with the greatest flexibility will be the most
consistently successful influencer.

6.   Behavioural flexibility provides the maximum opportunity for eventual success.

Chapter 9

Handling resistance

One can stand still in a flowing stream, but not in the world of men. Japanese proverb

Influencing is like a horse race. The first part is usually easy, then come the hurdles. You will inevitably meet some resistance to your proposals and this chapter shows how to recognize and handle objections and resistance.

Why do people resist the influence of others?

Think back to a time when you were close to agreeing a proposal then, for some reason, you became disillusioned with it and pulled out of the deal at the last minute. The chances are that you did not tell the other person why you had changed your mind. It may have been embarrassing to tell them. Quite often, resistance to influence is an intangible 'something' which went wrong. It need not relate to the nature of the offer. It may not be the costs involved. Not even the time frame. It could be something as simple as 'service'—or lack of it.

Take this example. A friend of mine, Chris, was keen to

buy his wife a second-hand car. He worked in the city and during his lunch breaks spent some time doing the rounds of the car showrooms. Eventually, one Friday, he found exactly the car he was looking for—a one-owner Volkswagen with sunroof, radio and in a colour he knew his wife would love. That weekend he took the money out of his bank and went with Anne to the showroom. After ten minutes they both left—without the car! Why did this happen? The car was the right one, the money was available, Anne wanted a car. What was it that came between their real needs and their willingness to make a decision to buy? Something took place which put them off buying. It was the service they received (or complete lack of service).

They walked into the showroom, keen and eager to go ahead, but there was no one in sight. They waited around for five minutes. Still no sign of a salesperson. When she did arrive, the saleswoman knew nothing of Chris's earlier visit, nor could she find the documents he had completed. 'Can you come back a bit later? The manager's out to lunch but should be back around 2.30.' They did buy a car the following week but it was not a Volkswagen nor was it from that dealer. Probably the motor dealer had no idea why the car remained unsold—why Chris's excitement of Friday turned sour on Saturday.

Whenever someone tries to influence us we are forced to make decisions. When we do this we make a mental journey. This can take just a few seconds or might take hours, days or weeks to complete. However long the journey takes the outcome will always be a decision to go ahead or not.

The journey to 'yes'

The journey to 'yes' is one we all take when we make decisions and follow a path which has seven clearly identifiable signposts along the way.

Step one: Interest

Our interest in an idea or proposition must be caught and maintained from the start. Interest can range from passing a shop window and noting an item which catches our eye, reading the headline in an advertisement, hearing a friend talk enthusiastically about a recent experience, or becoming aware of new trends or fashions. Whatever it is, something or someone must grab our attention and hold it long enough for us to feel the need to move on to:

Step two: Needs and wants

Now our attention has been attracted we start to ask ourselves a number of questions. Do I want this? How will I benefit? When we have satisfied ourselves (or deluded ourselves?) that we need or want what's on offer we ask ourselves more detailed questions and move on to:

Step three: Finding out

This is the critical stage when we check that the idea being suggested will fulfil certain criteria. These may include outlay, value for money, size, colour, quality, length of life, serviceability and so on. Also we may consider at this stage how other people will react. If we go ahead what effect will that decision have on others? When we have received appropriate answers to most of these questions we move on to:

Step four: Desire

You have convinced yourself that you need it, it fits all your criteria—and now you want it. You have to have it. Even this is not the final step.

Step five: Weighing it up

It is here that you attempt an objective analysis of the ultimate value of the idea or proposal. You weigh up and balance your desire against the costs to reach a measure of the value-for-money this idea will bring. You may decide to re-examine alternative proposals or solutions before committing. And for many this can be crunch time if costs outweigh desire making the proposal attractive but impossible.

Step six: Saying 'yes'

Even at this stage we do not always say 'yes' immediately. Perhaps we have to consult others before we can commit to the proposal. Possibly there are implementation plans which need to be drawn up and agreed. Some people want just one more night to sleep on it.

Step seven: Yes! I made a really good decision

So important, step seven. The need to verify our decision or to reassure ourselves is very powerful. A colleague told me recently that he had bought his girl friend a handbag in a souk in Istanbul. After much haggling he was satisfied with the eventual deal. Or so he thought. Down the road he spotted a shop selling identical bags and he was driven by some unknown demon to 'just pop in to check that the deal was worthwhile'. He received the confirmation he sought and went back to his hotel a happy man. Whether he was duped or not is beside the point. He was finally comfortable with the decision he had taken.

Exercise

1. Recall a recent decision which you have made (even if it was a decision *not* to do something). Think back over the steps you took in arriving at your decision.

Interest What was it that first aroused your interest?

Needs and wants What were the specific needs and wants which seemed to be fulfilled by the proposition?

Finding out What questions did you ask in order to find out more about the idea?

Desire How did you justify the final decision to go ahead?

Weighing it up When faced with the possibility of saying 'yes' how did you equate value-for-money with your desire?

Saying 'yes' How did you arrive at 'yes'? Slowly and with care and deliberation? Instantly without further thought? Did you bring others into the decision?

When we are under pressure to make decisions many thoughts rush through our heads. Do I trust and believe the influencer? Do I need to change? Am I happy with the way things are? Why do I have to make my mind up right now? The proposition sounds fine now—but how will it stand up to scrutiny in six months, a year? And anyway I am not convinced that we can afford it.

Many decisions which we make in life cause these automatic defence mechanisms to come into play. Sometimes our early automatic responses are just holding mechanisms slipped in early to give us time to think things through. There are people who never make hasty decisions and there are others who hate to make decisions to change. People avoid making decisions for a variety of reasons. They may be afraid of the outcome or what their friends and colleagues will say about their judgement. They may be too embarrassed to tell you why they cannot say 'yes' to your idea.

Using inappropriate words

There are certain words or phrases which can create almost instant resistance in other people. The lie detector is based on Jung's original word association test for discovering the nature of unconscious complexes. A list of one hundred words is read out to the person being tested. They are asked to respond to each word with the first word that comes into their head. Most of the words read out are neutral and evoke neutral responses. But certain key words are introduced which relate to subjects over which conflict can arise. An unusual association or lengthy delay gives clues to the testee's complexes.

Words, their context and the ways in which they are evaluated is a highly subjective area which remains under study by psychologists around the world. For our purposes let's examine a number of words and phrases which will universally create resistance in those we are attempting to influence. Benjamin Franklin had a useful strategy for telling people what he thought while still maintaining rapport with them:

> I develop the habit of expressing myself in terms of modest diffidence, never using when I advanced anything that may possibly be disputed the words 'certainly', 'undoubtedly' or any others that give the air of positiveness to an opinion, but rather say I conceive or apprehend a thing to be so and so: 'It appears to me' or 'I should

not think it so or so for such and such reasons'; or 'I imagine it to be so' or 'It is so, if I am not much mistaken'.

This habit I believe has been of great advantage to me when I have had occasion to inculcate my opinion and persuade men into measures that I have been time to time engaged in promoting.

Interactions between people seem to be at their most effective when emotions are positive. When influencing others your constant goal should be always to avoid generating negative emotional responses—the ones you are trying to develop are either positive or at least neutral.

Here are other words which are almost guaranteed to produce a negative response:

- But
  'I agree with you entirely, but. . . .' What does this mean? You are saying: 'I do not agree with you entirely.' Exactly the opposite of the words used. The word 'but' is arguably one of the most destructive words in English. Its use immediately reverses the main message and creates instantaneous resistance in the listener.

  In future try substituting 'and' every time you feel the urge to use 'but'. In the above example your words would now read: 'I agree with you entirely and there is another thing I agree with . . .'

- I disagree
  And well you might—but never tell people you disagree. Say instead: 'I can see your point of view and I think there may be an even more effective way of . . .'

- I assume
  Don't assume anything. Even if you assume correctly there are people who will totally disagree with your assumptions just for the sheer hell of it. Try something softer: 'If I am right in thinking that . . .' This leaves open the possibility that your 'assumption' could be incorrect and offers people the option to correct you. But they very rarely do if you soften the phrase.

What's the meaning of this?

Apart from simple words like 'but' and 'if', the following phrases can convey a very negative meaning to a listener:

- There are a few disadvantages.
- There is only a small work volume increase.
- I cannot pretend that there won't be a few delays.
- I hope you're not too busy to see me.
- It isn't going to cost a fortune.
- The meeting wasn't a complete waste of time.
- With respect . . .
- I hear what you say.
- Feel free to say no.
- I don't know how to put this.
- I bet you're going to think . . .

Who owns the decision in placing value on these statements—the deliverer (you) or the receiver? How can you improve these statements and be sure that the message you have decided to give is the one which is received?

Insufficient information

Often, resistance to ideas or proposals is the result of insufficient information. Quite often, as others are talking, we hear only a portion of what they are saying. This is not necessarily a result of not listening. It is frequently because we have allowed ourselves to become distracted. Take this dialogue for example:

> Influencer: 'I think you will find that the new system will work particularly well for people who have just started with the company. Also, how many times have you asked yourself "What will it cost us in lost time and lost orders if we do not update the system?" So, what do you think? Shall we go ahead?'
> You: 'I think we ought to give it time. I have rather a lot on my plate at the moment so come back and tell

me again when the current recruitment campaign is completed. Perhaps in three months which will give me time to complete the induction training course.'

Among the fifty or so words which the influencer uttered was the phrase 'people who have just started with the company'. Unknown to the influencer this phrase was all you heard. It rang loud bells for you as you are preoccupied with the current recruitment drive. All kinds of images poured into your head: advertisements which had to be booked, media selected, who would be able to help you interview and so on. Meanwhile the influencer is convinced that you heard the key words 'what will it cost in lost time and lost orders?'

Lack of conviction

Some people resist influence from the outset. Nobody, nowhere, nohow is going to influence them to change. So there! They start and finish the process with a closed mind. There could be a number of reasons for this:

- They don't like the influencer (poor rapport skills).
- They have already sampled the idea and it failed.
- They know someone else who sampled the idea and had a bad experience.
- They have already incorporated your proposal into their system.
- They don't see a need for what you are suggesting.

In the following dialogue between you and the influencer other forces may be at work. Forces which also prevent a decision being made.

Influencer: 'I am sure you'll agree that what I'm suggesting will save you time and money. So, shall we go ahead?'

You: 'Hhmm. I think I'd rather wait a while. Maybe you could come back to me in a couple of months.'

In this case you are simply unconvinced that the proposal will save time or money. You do not need more time to think it through—you need more convincing.

Anticipating objections and resistance

Imagine for a moment that you are a jockey; a good rider with years of experience. Today, you are entered in a brand new race on an unfamiliar course. Having arrived later than expected, you find you have no time to 'walk the course' and see for yourself the bends and jumps which lie ahead. You mount, grasp the reins and the starting gate flies up. It's a straightforward race, like most others—normal bends, good going, no real competition. You are ahead by about three lengths; keep this up and the prize is yours. You approach the fences—only half a dozen, the usual thing. Over the first three without even noticing them—now for the fourth. Your horse slows his approach, half turns from the jump, then makes an attempt. Feet graze the top, a stumbled landing and you are thrown. Your race is over. You stand at the edge of the course watching the other jockeys sweep by.

Objections are the 'fences' you will certainly encounter during your race to influence people. If you are ready for them you will be able easily to overcome these hurdles and you will achieve your goal. However, if you fail to handle even one objection, major or minor, you will also fail to influence other people.

Using your empathy

Before beginning to influence anyone, put yourself in their position. Empathize: imagine what you would think about the proposal if it was being made to you. What doubts, fears, misgivings or objections would you have? Perhaps you might have concerns about the financing of the proposal? What about the timing—would you be ready to decide to go ahead on the spot, or would you want to think it over? Would anyone else be involved in the decision process? Your boss, partner, financial adviser? Would other options be available to you? Would you want to take time to look at these before you make your decision? Perhaps you feel happy with the present position and don't see the need for a change?

By empathizing, putting yourself in the other person's position, you will be able to see most objections long before they arise—and you'll have your answer ready. It may even be possible to answer the objection before it arises:

> Chris, I realize that you're concerned about the bottom line and, yes, my solution does seem a bit expensive at first glance. However, I can reassure you . . .

But—a word of warning. Ask yourself this question: 'In anticipating the objection, raising it myself and then answering it, will I create unnecessary doubts or fears in the mind of the person I am trying to influence?' Sometimes it is better to let sleeping dogs lie; if you don't acknowledge the problem, it may never be raised. Either way, you must decide how you will deal with anticipated objections and walk the course before you construct your argument and enter the race.

Preparing to answer objections: The three rules

There are very few areas in our lives where planning fails to pay. Many people are impulsive, they do not plan ahead—never mind if they encounter problems, these can always be dealt with as they arise. Treat planning as an investment. Care and thought invested at this stage will invariably pay dividends in the long term. Here are three simple rules—if you follow these you need never worry again about what you should do if the other person says 'No' to your proposals.

Rule one: Have an answer to the objection

I was once accompanying a salesman, Mike, on his sales calls to see what training he needed. To start with, he did quite well. Then, towards the end of the conversation, the buyer made a simple statement: 'We are very happy with our present supplier.' There was a long silence. Mike looked at the ground, then the ceiling—finally at me! He mumbled a long and rambling reply, which the buyer didn't accept, and a few minutes later we left. As we got back into the car, Mike turned to me and said: 'I knew he was going to come out with that one—I just knew it.' I bit my tongue and said nothing. It had not been a good morning and to utter my thoughts at that point would not have helped matters. I wanted to scream: 'For Heaven's sake, Mike! How can you go into that man's office *knowing* what he was going to say . . . and not have an answer ready?'

Always have a polished response to any and every objection you think may come up. Rehearse it, remember it, try it out on a friend and obtain feedback from them. Did your reply make sense and was it consistent?

Rule two: Keep your answer brief

How do *you* feel about people who give you long, rambling answers to your concerns and queries? Most people feel bored and frustrated. Some even feel that they are being duped. Give just the right amount of information needed to respond to the objection—no more, no less. Try to avoid repeating your points. Write down answers to any objections you anticipate. This will help to clarify your thinking. Put the written answer to one side for a while; on reviewing it you will find that you can edit it and make it a shorter and crisper answer.

Rule three: Obtain agreement that the objection has been answered

Really successful persuaders do this all the time. Just because *you* think you have dealt with an objection, it doesn't mean that the other person thinks so too. Doubts may still linger in their mind, they may have misunderstood your answer. Ask the following question outright: 'Have I answered your question/solved the problem/convinced you, or would you like more information?' An alternative question might be: 'Before we continue, are you satisfied that I have answered that point you have just raised?' By asking this direct question you force the other person to agree, or disagree, at a crucial point in the dialogue. If you don't ask this question how will you know for certain that you have answered their objection? How can you be sure that it won't arise again, perhaps at the end of the conversation grouped neatly under the umbrella statement: 'I'd like to think it over, there are still a few points I want to consider'?

How to recognize the different types of objection

Although we talk loosely about people resisting our proposals or raising an 'objection' that we couldn't answer, there is no such thing as 'an objection'. When people resist a proposition, they usually raise one of four different types of objection.

1. A condition

A condition is a watertight, copper-bottomed reason why the other person cannot agree to do what you are asking them. There is no way round a condition. The three main conditions you are likely to encounter are:

- I already have what you are suggesting. I am not aware of any need.
- I cannot make the decision on my own (although good planning should have revealed this earlier).
- It is against company policy/the rules/the law.

Notice that the objections 'I do not have any money' and

'It is the wrong time', 'I want to think it over', are not included in the list of conditions. All of these standard objections can be countered with practice.

When you hear a condition and are *absolutely certain* that it is a condition, back off. Stop trying to influence, don't push any harder. It is more productive to go away and re-think your proposal; there may be a way around the problem. Talk to other people, hear their views and experiences and try again later. Don't force your views on people when they clearly can't make a decision. Sometimes it takes more courage to back out of a losing situation than it does to battle on without success. Remember the old prayer:

> Give us the serenity to accept what cannot be changed, the courage to change what should be changed, and the wisdom to distinguish the one from the other. (Reinhold Niebuhr, quoted in Hopkins, Tom, 1982, *How To Master the Art of Selling*.)

2. A misunderstanding

Often people will object to a proposal because they misunderstand some aspect. It could be that circumstances have altered since they first heard about your ideas. Perhaps you have altered your proposition to include features which were not previously there. The misunderstanding is easy to recognize and simple to resolve.

> **Them:** *'I can't possibly make a decision today. I need time to think over what you're saying'.*
> **You:** *'That isn't a problem. Please take your time—the project doesn't start for another six weeks, so you have plenty of time. Meanwhile this will allow us the opportunity to study more closely how it will affect production control'.*

The other person thinks they are objecting, you recognize it as a misunderstanding—you clear it up. Simple, isn't it?

3. Excuses and stalling tactics

For most of us excuses and stalling tactics can be among the most difficult of objections to deal with because they are also the hardest to identify. How can you tell whether a person really means

'I can't afford it.'
'I have to talk to my partner.'
'It's the wrong time of year.'?

These could all be genuine—but equally they could all be excuses.

The following dialogue is typical of one where the other person is desperately seeking an excuse—for whatever reason, they just don't feel able or ready to say 'No'. Notice the give-away signals which suggest that these might be excuses.

You: *'OK. We've taken a fresh look at the costings—why don't we aim for the 17th as a start date?'*
Them: *'Er... No, that's no good. I'm a bit tied up that week.'*
You: *'No problem, how about week commencing the 21st?'*
Them: *'Ah... I'm on holiday that week.'*
You: *'That's OK. Your assistant, Jo, will be around. She and I can start to install the system while you're away.'*
Them: *'Yes, but Jo's not too familiar with the details...'*
You: *'In that case we could get Chris, the Systems Manager, to help.'*
Them: *'Um... I don't really want Chris to be involved at this stage...'*

And so on and so on and so on. Every time you suggest what seems to be a perfectly acceptable solution to the problems they raise it is immediately countered with an apparently equally logical argument. Did you spot those give-away signals?

- liberal use of 'ers', 'ums' and 'ahs';

- a different 'reason' was given each time you thought you had solved the problem;
- their use of the phrase 'Yes, but . . .'.

There is one simple reason why you are hearing excuses rather than logical objections: the other person is unconvinced. This is serious. If you are successfully to influence others, to gain their commitment, then conviction is of paramount importance.

What are the reasons why they may remain unconvinced?

1. They do not see a need for what you are suggesting.
2. You have not bothered to establish their needs.
3. They do see they have a need but remain unconvinced of the benefits you have outlined.
4. They do not see how they might gain from the benefits you have described.
5. You have misinterpreted their needs and are talking about the wrong benefits.
6. You have not developed sufficient rapport or empathy.
7. You appear to them as a pushy sales type.
8. They do not believe what you say.
9. They are naturally cautious and always look hard before they leap.
10. They never had any intention of accepting your suggestions.

Each possible reason is potentially serious. It may be a case of 'back to the drawing board', to reappraise your original strategy. Talk to others about your problem. Perhaps they have experienced similar problems with this person and can throw light on your difficulties. Devise a suitable role play which accurately reflects the issues *and run the role play with you playing the part of the person to be convinced.* This can prove invaluable as you are likely to experience some of the feelings which they are experiencing. This is empathy—putting yourself in someone else's position.

4. Genuine objections to your idea or proposal

If the objections you are hearing are not conditions, mis-understandings or excuses—then they are almost certainly genuine. Real objections or resistances are easier to overcome because they spring from reality, or from the heart.

Sometimes we object because we seek more information or reassurance. How often have you left a shop having bought a product or service which you thought was rather costly? At the pit of your stomach lies a knot of guilt or self-doubt. 'Should I have bought this? Can I justify it? What will my partner/friend/colleague say?' This feeling is quite common. It is called 'buyer's remorse' and simply means that the sales assistant failed to outweigh cost concerns with appropriate benefits.

So when someone says 'I think it costs too much' this may well be a plea for more information, more benefit statements which will help the other person draw up their own checklist of reasons to use when they in turn are asked, 'Why did you say yes to the idea?'

Here is a list of typical objections along with classic responses. But beware: classic textbook responses are all very well but they swiftly lose their currency. As more people use them, more hear them—and they wear a bit thin after a while. So as you read and learn the classic replies begin to be aware of how you will adjust these to suit you and the circumstances when you first begin successfully to use them.

Cost

Ask any professional salesperson 'What is the objection you hear most' and they'll reply: cost/money/budget/too expensive/too cheap/no terms available and so on.

Here are some approaches you could take. A mathematical approach provides a simple and useful framework or mnemonic on which to base your responses.

Plus–Minus–Multiply–Divide

The Plus objection: 'Your idea is *more expensive* than the existing method.'

Answer: 'Yes, it is more expensive at first glance; however, you do gain *additional* benefits . . .' (Plus highlights the extras gained.)

The Minus objection: 'The existing method is *less expensive* than your proposal.'

Answer: 'Yes, you are right, it is *cheaper*; however, it *does not provide* the following benefits . . .' (Minus spotlights any benefits they may forego.)

The Multiply objection: 'Wow! That's a lot more than I expected.'

Answer: 'Yes, it is quite pricey. But remember that we are a *quality* company and you would expect to pay a little extra for our reputation.' (Multiply reminds them of hidden or intangible extras such as quality or reputation. The quality is remembered long after the price is forgotten.)

The Divide objection: 'That's quite a bit more than I thought it would come to.'

You: 'How much were you thinking of paying?'

Them: 'Oh, about £400.'

You: 'So as your investment in my idea will come to around £425 you are concerned about £25, is that right?'

Them: 'Yes.'

You: 'Well, that shouldn't present too much of a problem. The expected life will be well over five years. But if we spread that difference over just five years what are we talking about? Only £5 a year. The cost of a few litres of petrol.' (Divide reduces the difference between expected expenditure and actual down to the lowest common denominator. Then for good measure this already much reduced figure is compared to a typical everyday outgoing such as petrol, beer, or even bread.)

Time

No time, too much time, wrong time. However it is expressed time is often cited as a 'reason' for not making a decision.

Objection: 'It is too early.'
You: 'When will be a more appropriate time to go ahead?'
Them: 'Oh, not for another couple of months.'
You: (reframing) 'That's fine. The delay will give us an opportunity to double-check things and give you greater peace of mind.'

Objection: 'It is too late. We already made the decision to change last week.'
You: (reframing) 'I am sorry we missed the boat this time around but it is encouraging to hear that you do review these things from time to time. When do you think will be the next time to review?'
Them: 'Probably in about a year.'
You: (reframing) 'Fine. We can use the time usefully by refining the idea even more to dovetail with your needs. Tell me—when do you think this will come up for review?'
Them: 'Not sure.'
You: (SuperQuestion) 'I understand. But if you did have an idea when it will come up for review when do think that might be?'

NB. Whatever time or date they give you *make sure you submit your proposals earlier than they say.* If you don't you can be sure someone else will!

Exercise—Handling resistance to your ideas or proposals

List overleaf the objections which concern you most. How will you answer them in the future?

Continued
1.
2.
3.
4.

Force field analysis

Influencing for change means shifting the status quo. Quite often there is an unusual or innovative solution lurking somewhere—if only people would agree to do something about it! There are frequently problems in organizations, departments, clubs or families which, if nothing is done to bring about change, will remain as permanent problems. This is because the problem can be viewed as a balance of forces which are working in opposite directions. You have identified the problem and are anxious to promote change (the driving forces necessary to resolve the problem). Unfortunately there are very often forces of equal strength which may inhibit change (restraining forces).

A 'force field' consists of these two categories of force— the drivers versus the restrainers. If an analysis reveals that there are more restrainers than drivers, then the status quo is likely to remain. But change this balance in favour of more (or more convincing) drivers and you are on the road to change and success. However, an increase in the driving forces is apt to bring about an increase in the restraining forces. Permanent change requires the removal of all significant restrainers.

Force field analysis is just one of the many approaches to problem solving. It lends itself particularly well to the process of influencing for change as it encourages both sides to analyse whether it is logical or desirable to allow things to stay the same. For you, the influencer, it is vital to be armed with as many drivers as you can muster. You can be certain that others will have a rich selection of restrainers to counter-balance your arguments.

How to construct a force field analysis

1. Write the target or desired state in a box in the centre of the page and draw a line from this box down the middle of the page.

> Reduced staff turnover

2. Brainstorm the potential drivers. This is a particularly fruitful way of accumulating a devastating list to shore up your case. When you brainstorm drivers:

   - enlist the help of a handful of creative friends;
   - aim for quantity rather than quality;
   - refrain from judging or evaluating at this stage;
   - don't forget to brainstorm the restrainers—be fully aware of the other side's arguments.

On the left-hand side list the drivers and draw arrows up to the line for each driving force.

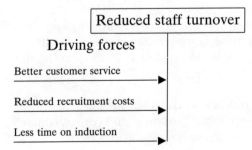

3. On the right-hand side list the restraining forces and
    draw arrows up to the line.

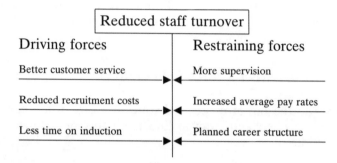

The length of the arrows can be used to indicate stronger
and weaker forces, e.g. the longer the arrow, the stronger the
force.

Now you have a tighter grasp of the forces opposing
change (or problem resolution) move on to stage two of the
force field analysis—implementation.

- Strengthen the drivers, weaken the restrainers.
- Select drivers or restrainers which are the easiest to
  change with the greatest payoff.
- Devise an action plan and a strategy for influencing
  change through force fielding.
- Will your strategy help you achieve your objective?
- If not, which drivers or restrainers will?

There are many problem areas on which we can successfully
bring our individual influence to bear. Assuming that the
solution will be reached automatically or by others who
have greater knowledge or superior status can be a big
mistake. How often have you seen a new system installed
which is later modified, sometimes quite radically? When
you talk to the people whose job it is to operate the new
system they say things such as:

'We knew it wouldn't work from the start.'
You enquire, reasonably: 'So why didn't you say something?'
They respond: 'Because nobody asked us, that's why!'

Exercise—Force field analysis

1. Suppose you are anxious to influence the outcome of a community meeting. A number of local residents are meeting to discuss the pros and cons of asking the local authority to bring in a residents' parking scheme. At present valuable street parking spots are being taken early in the morning by people who then walk into the town centre for their work. Very often they do not return until late afternoon. This makes it difficult if not impossible for local residents to park anywhere close to home. In turn this is awkward if you have to unload from your car or if you have small children.
2. You recognize that about half of those present at this evening's meeting will be against any residents' parking scheme as it will cost them money and they feel that urban parking should always be free.
3. Brainstorm all the drivers you can—anything which will serve to back your argument. Concentrate on three or four powerful drivers and think of ways in which you might add further value to their power in the forthcoming argument.
4. Now do the same with the restrainers (you already have one: 'It will cost us money'). Which restrainers are the most powerful? How can you weaken them? Can you lessen their impact by using one or more of your drivers as a counter-argument?

We have already seen that it is necessary to gain other peoples' commitment to change if the outcome is not to be sabotaged or weakened. Although force field analysis is only one of many ways of tackling a problem there are many areas where it could be useful to you, the influencer.

1. Systems problems
2. Company policy issues
3. Improvements to customer service
4. Recruitment and selection issues

5.   Personal or family problems
6.   Changes of direction in life or career.

Reframing

You glance out of the window and notice that it is raining. How typical! You have the day off tomorrow—and it rains. This always seems to happen to you. You make detailed plans and they fall apart—all because of the weather. Huh!!

See how easy it is to allow ourselves to enter into a downward spiral which results in feelings of disempowerment. Does this need to happen? First we tend to blame our feelings on the weather. 'I'd be a lot happier if the sun was shining.' In fact we are *allowing ourselves to feel this way* because of some outside event. It is not the event itself which causes feelings.

Secondly there are many ways of looking at things. Events mean quite different things to different people. Question: who will feel positively delighted that it is raining? Farmers, water authorities, fishermen, gardeners.

When you attempt to influence others they will often use some negative-sounding event as an excuse or apparent reason for not agreeing with you.

'We can't go ahead with the new software because I have three new people starting on Monday.'

How could you re-state (or reframe) this statement in order to show its positive side? How about: 'That could actually be a good time to install. The three new people won't get used to the old system only to find it suddenly replaced.'

Reframing negative words

Some people don't need a whole phrase or sentence to help enhance their feelings of helplessness. For many of us just a word here and there is sufficient. All of the following words fit into this category:

Angry   Anxious
Disappointed   Embarrassed
Fearful   Hurt
Insulted   Overwhelmed
Rejected   Scared
Stressed   Terrible

Let's take them one by one and reframe them to provide a more positive or resourceful outlook on life:

Angry = Disenchanted
Anxious = A little concerned
Disappointed = Surprised
Embarrassed = Stimulated
Fearful = Curious
Hurt = Bothered
Insulted = Misunderstood
Overwhelmed = Challenged
Rejected = Overlooked
Scared = Excited
Stressed = Energized
Terrible = Unusual

Now reframe these typical negative power words:

Difficulties ....
Dissatisfaction ....
Worry ....
Fear ....
Concern ....
Problems ....
Doubt ....
Won't ....
Can't ....
Loss ....

You may be thinking that taken out of context some of these one-word reframes may sound a little insubstantial. But put them in a real-life situation, use them and see the difference they can make to an otherwise unproductive conversation.

Reframing criteria

When you are asking people to make a decision you are also asking them to measure your proposition against their criteria for deciding. Criteria can be divided into:

- tangible: cost; volume; quantity; time;
- intangible: better looking; more user friendly; up to date; feels right.

Logical or emotional, tangible or intangible, other people's criteria are hard to argue against. But it is possible, through reframing, to change their definition by asking the question 'What else could this mean?'

For example: 'I can't decide right now. I'll have to wait two months for the new budget to come on stream' can be reframed by responding: 'Great. That two-month period will give us plenty of time to dry-run the system and ensure that it is entirely free of bugs.'

To reframe apparently negative criteria ask yourself: *'What else could this mean?'*

Exercise—Reframing resistance

Here are some negative statements and words which you may encounter.

Write alongside each a statement or word which you feel could reframe the original in a more positive light. Work quickly and do not labour over any one example. If a reframe does not come easily to mind move on to the next statement and go back later to complete any which remain.

At the end there is space to add a few of your own favourite words or phrases.

> *Continued*
>
> Frustrated
> It's the wrong colour
> I can't afford it
> It will take too long
> Insecure
> Furious
> More user friendly
> Cheaper
> ☺
> ☺
> ☺

Summary

1. By understanding the steps we take when arriving at a decision, you will also be able to understand the fragility of persuasive communication.
2. Avoid the inappropriate words and phrases which can create unwanted, unconscious reflex negative responses.
3. Make certain you have provided full information and proof.
4. Anticipate and deal in advance with likely objections or resistance. Use your empathy to imagine what you would think about the proposal if it was being made to you.
5. Always have an answer to likely resistance. Keep it short and get agreement that the objection has been answered before moving on.
6. Learn to detect those behaviours which signal excuses or stalling tactics.
7. Use force field analysis to identify drivers or restrainers. Amplify the drivers, weaken the restrainers.
8. Form the habit of reframing negative attitudes or statements.

Chapter 10

Obtaining a decision

With too much knowledge for the sceptic side,
With too much weakness for the stoic's pride,
He hangs between; in doubt to act or rest;
Alexander Pope

People often hover on the brink of decision, needing a gentle nudge to help them take that final step. This chapter analyses why we avoid asking for decisions and offers a variety of ways by which you can extract a 'Yes'.

The phrase 'influencing for change' implies a shift from one position to another, from 'No' to 'Yes', from 'Yes' to 'No', from inactivity to activity—a measurable departure from the status quo. In whatever way you define the changes you seek the result will usually be tangible or measurable. And unless the person you are influencing offers an unconditional 'Yes' to your proposals you will need to do or say something which will generate a positive decision.

This moment, the moment of deciding, is one of the most critical in the influencing process. For many people it is anathema to have to ask: 'Shall we go ahead, then?' Why is this so often the case? There are several reasons why you may be reluctant to push for a decision, some of which are quite understandable—others not so.

Why some people avoid asking for a decision

- Psychological reasons: Consciously or unconsciously you may feel that this is somehow demeaning, intrusive, manipulative, unethical or deceptive. Surely, you say to yourself, surely if the other person wants to proceed they will say so in their own good time.
- Structural authority: Your own position within the organization may be quite low down the pecking order creating a real or perceived deterrent from asking for a decision.
- Sapiential or expert authority: The person you are influencing may not necessarily possess structural authority but they are regarded as having knowledge, expertise or wisdom. Your perception of the other person 'knowing more than I do' may present a further weakening of intent on your part.
- Moral authority: The person who you are influencing conducts themselves in such a moral, just or virtuous fashion making you feel that any pressure from you might be regarded as unseemly or distasteful.
- Dynastic authority: The Godfather Syndrome. The other person may be held in such awe by others within the family or group that it is socially unacceptable or simply not done to be seen to put any kind of pressure on them.

Why people delay making a decision

Imagine that you are reading a newspaper. Suddenly your eye is caught by an advertisement—an illustration or the promise contained in the headline has intrigued you sufficiently to stop reading a news item. You turn to the advertisement. You read it and perhaps read it again, just to be certain. Yes, you think, it sounds promising. I must do something about this. At that moment the phone rings and you put your newspaper down. Later you pick up the paper. 'Now, where was I?' you say, turning to another news item. All positive thoughts you may have had about responding to the advertisement have evaporated. Later you might wonder vaguely where it was you saw that advertisement but the moment has passed and despite your good intentions you never reach the final decision to do something about what you had read. (Possibly this is why so many advertisements include phrases like: Hurry while stocks last; Rush me your catalogue; Offer closes end of May. Or why there is a coupon in the bottom corner of the advertisement with a broken line around it and a drawing of a pair of scissors, just in case you are a complete idiot and are unfamiliar with how to respond!)

The road to Hell is paved with good intentions.

Exercise—Delaying a decision

1. Think back to a time when you were being asked to make a decision. Recall the doubts and fears which filled your mind. Put yourself right back to the moment when you finally said 'No'.

2. What was it exactly which prevented you from agreeing?

3. What would have had to take place for you to agree?

The following are some reasons why people may consider putting off the evil moment of decision:

1. They do not have sufficient faith in you, your organiz-
    ation/department/social group.
2. They do not fully understand the implications of your
    proposal.
3. They do not see how they will benefit from the ideas
    you put forward.
4. There are other possible options open to them.
5. Lethargy: they are content with the status quo—thank
    you very much.

In short—they are unconvinced.

I'd like to think it over

'I would like to give your proposals a bit of thought
before I decide what to do.' This is the classic stalling tactic.
We have all encountered it at some time in our lives and
said it to others. But what do those words 'I'd like to think
it over' suggest? Clearly the other person is still unconvinced
or they would probably say 'Yes' without too much hesitation.

There is a right way and a wrong way of dealing with 'I
want to think about it'. Let's examine the wrong way. It is
tempting to ask simply and straightforwardly:

'Why do you need to think it over?' or perhaps,
'What is it you want to think about?'

By all means ask these questions but when you do notice
how they will almost certainly produce a response like: 'Oh,
nothing really. I just didn't reach my present position by
making hasty decisions' or 'I always believe it helps to sleep
on things'. How does that help? It doesn't. You are back
where you started and none the wiser.

What do you need to know before you can deal with this
indecision? You need to know specifically *what it is that is
preventing them* from making a decision.

Now for the right way. Whenever anyone says 'I want to
think about it' the dialogue might go something like this:

'I agree it is a difficult decision' (empathizing) 'but obviously there is something you don't understand or are unhappy about . . .' (Do not pause here) ' . . . is it the time frame?'

'No, I am quite happy with that.'

'Well, is it perhaps the funding?'

'No, not really. I am confident that we can fund it through the production budget.'

'So is it the proposed project team?'

'Yes—I am not happy with Joan Parsons' involvement. We used her on the new postal system and found her to be very slow.'

'Is Joan's involvement the only thing which prevents you from making a decision?'

'Yes, I think everything else is fine.'

'So if I can guarantee that she won't be on this team you'd be happy to go ahead?'

'Yes.'

Questionnaire: Your preferred decision-making criteria

Whenever someone tries to influence us the important critical question is: 'Will we say "Yes" to their proposition?' This questionnaire will help you to understand what influences your decisions and can throw light on the ways in which others like to make their decisions.

Read each question then circle the ③ most appropriate answers:

A. When you choose a new car which factors are most important to you?

1. The price	6. Overall size of car
2. The dealer's reputation	7. The design
3. Plenty of extras	8. Popular model
4. The location of the dealer	9. Long-term warranty available
5. Reliable make of car	10. Helpful staff

B. When you pick a restaurant which of these influences your choice?

1. The basic cost of a meal
2. How well known the chef is
3. Plenty of variety on the menu
4. How far away the restaurant is
5. Dependable food
6. How big the restaurant is
7. Its decor
8. Fashionable
9. Satisfaction assured
10. Cheerful waiting staff

C. If you were thinking of joining a new company which factors would influence you the most?

1. The salary
2. Its reputation in its field
3. Offers varied career paths
4. How close to home is it
5. Quality of goods/services made
6. The size of the organization
7. How modern the office/factory/shop is
8. A nationally/internationally known company
9. A contract of employment
10. A good crowd to work with

D. When selecting a holiday hotel which factors would you consider the most important?

1. The overall price
2. The reputation of the hotel
3. Plenty of things to do and see
4. How long the journey will take
5. How many stars the hotel has
6. Large/medium/small hotel
7. Attractive design
8. Famous place to stay
9. Agent is a member of IATA
10. Efficient and helpful hotel staff

E. If you were choosing a house, what would influence you the most?

1. Its price
2. District has a good reputation
3. Its potential for development
4. Its distance from facilities
5. Well-built property
6. How many rooms it has
7. Its interior design
8. It is a fashionable area to live in
9. Has received a good survey
10. Pleasant neighbours

F. Suppose you had to live in another country. Which of these aspects appeal the most?

1. The cost of living
2. Respected in world community
3. Offers more choices in life-style
4. Accessible by sea and air
5. Quality of life
6. Population total
7. Beautiful countryside
8. Your friends will love to come and stay
9. A very safe place to live and work
10. Friendly inhabitants

G. You are choosing a school for your child. Which criteria are most important to you?

1. The fees
2. School's academic record
3. A wide curriculum is available
4. How far it is from your home
5. Best teaching available
6. Number of pupils
7. Modern/traditional buildings
8. It is a famous school
9. It is a safe, caring environment
10. Teachers are approachable

H. When you shop in a department store, which of these aspects appeal most?

1. Its prices
2. Its reputation
3. There is a lot of choice
4. Easy to get to
5. Top-grade goods on sale
6. How large it is
7. Up-to-date interior
8. Well-known, exclusive store
9. You can return unsuitable items
10. Shop assistants are helpful and cheerful

Scoring

Add up the frequency with which you chose the numbered suggestions and record your totals on the scale below.

Choice 1 —— (Money)
Choice 2 —— (Reputation)
Choice 3 —— (Variety)
Choice 4 —— (Location)
Choice 5 —— (Quality)

Choice 6 —— (Size)
Choice 7 —— (Looks)
Choice 8 —— (Popularity)
Choice 9 —— (Safe decision)
Choice 10 —— (People factors)

Interpretation

The words used in each of your choices were synonyms of each other (e.g. cost of living:fees:price:discounts). Most people find two or three themes recur whenever they are forced to examine a range of criteria in order to make a choice. Surprisingly this can apply to people as well as 'things'. We choose our friends and relationships in the same way as we select a car, an item in a shop or a holiday.

The questionnaire offers you only ten choices but there are many more common themes which can be important to people when they make a decision. Everyone has their own set of 'hot buttons'. Once developed these motivators rarely change from decision to decision. If you buy your newspaper from a particular vendor because you like him, you might also live in an area because of the neighbours, or choose to work with a friendly group of people. The choices may seem to be different but in fact all can be seen as synonymous. Some buying motivations are listed below—alongside each are three synonyms, vague words which can mean the same things to different people.

Fast	Quick	Speedy	Saves time
Safe	Reliable	Dependable	Guaranteed
Cheap	Low cost	Inexpensive	Money saving
Reputable	Name	Image	Make
Well known	Advertised	Famous	Popular
Service	Helpful	Polite	Efficient
Convenient	Near	Easy	Opening hours
Looks	Shape	Size	Colour
Fashionable	Popular	Modern	Current
Prestigious	Classical	Enviable	First rate
Traditional	Old style	Dependable	Familiar
Varied	Choice	Alternatives	Not tied down
Friendly	Cheerful	Chatty	Comfortable
Performance	Reliability	Standards	Durability
Unique	Different	New	Leading edge
Comfortable	Reliable	Worry free	Peace of mind

Establishing decision criteria

Each of us has developed our preferred strategies for making decisions and a variety of (changing) criteria from which we can choose. It is important to consider this when we are seeking approval for our ideas or proposals. But how exactly can we elicit strategies or criteria from people who sometimes have only a vague idea themselves of what it is they are seeking? Short of giving everyone a questionnaire how can you establish what motivates them?

There are several approaches you can take, each depending on circumstances.

- Ask them to tell you what appealed to them about a similar decision they have already taken. What factors influenced their decision? Was it the cost? Or perhaps the time frame? Have they carried out a similar project in the past? If so, how successful was it? What made it so successful? (Perhaps it was not a success in which case find out what it was that prevented it from being a success. If they were dissatisfied discover why, what went wrong, what would they have preferred?)
- Encourage them to talk you through their preferred strategies. For example: 'When you decide to upgrade a system how do you usually go about it? Do you do this on your own, or after consulting others? Who else do you rely on for advice?'—and so on.
- Talk to people who know them well or those who work alongside them. Ask: Have you noticed how she goes about making decisions? Who does she usually consult? What seems to be uppermost in her mind as she goes about deciding?
- Ask: How will you decide whether my proposition is valid and will work for you?

When should you ask for a decision?

If I had a pound for every time I have been asked that question I would be extremely wealthy. There is of course no definitive answer. I was once asked by a Director of a company whose annual sales conference I was about to address: 'Tell 'em to close the sale early and often.' I did not oblige because I feel the old adage 'Always Be Closing— the ABC of persuasion' is fundamentally flawed.

Suppose you do ask for the decision early. Perhaps before all information has been absorbed, before you have explained the appropriate benefits, before all outstanding objections have been dealt with. Are they likely to provide a resounding 'Yes' at this stage?

You opt to ask for a decision as often as you can. The first time you ask the answer is 'No, I'm not ready to decide.' You ask again a bit later but they are still undecided. Each time you ask you are forcing them to question earlier refusals to commit. Asking too frequently can only reinforce original reasons for saying 'No' in the first place.

The right time to ask for a decision

So, assuming that you don't ask early and you avoid asking too often, when is the right time? The right time is when you start to receive signals that suggest the person you are trying to influence seems ready to make their decision. When we are mentally prepared to 'go ahead' we give out messages, some conscious, others unconscious. Successful influencers seem almost instinctively to know when to get a decision. Many years of practice may have provided them with foolproof but entirely unconscious skills in closing the conversation. If you are a novice or still uncertain of your abilities you will be consciously observing the other person and noticing what changes take place throughout your dialogue which suggest that now is the right time to ask for a decision.

There are two indications which will tell you that other people may be ready to decide.

Appropriate body language signals

Suppose you were buying a wristwatch for a friend's birthday and were unable to decide between three possible choices. Each watch had its own set of attributes, but was different. So difficult, this decision making. First you picked up one, then another. You put it down and picked up the first again. You thought you noticed a small blemish on the strap and rubbed it gently with your finger. No problem—it came off immediately. The shopkeeper would not need a masters degree in psychology to realize quite early on which of the watches on offer had already become your preferred choice.

The following are body language signals which may indicate that others are ready to make a final decision. Remember though that one swallow does not make a summer. It may take several signals—separately or in clusters—before you can be certain that it is the right time to go for a decision.

- Sitting or leaning forward
- Head up, good eye contact
- Stroking chin thoughtfully
- Nodding
- Smiling in agreement
- Making notes—especially ticking a list
- Knees apart
- Feet flat on floor
- Hands in open gesture (palms up)
- Coat unbuttoned
- Upward inflection in voice tone

Changes in body language   Apart from the many individual signals, you will also notice subtle (and not so subtle) changes in the other person's body language. Perhaps, when you first mentioned your ideas, the other person was sitting or leaning hard against the back of the chair, feet stretched out in front of them, ankles crossed. Their hands may have been closed or clasped in the shape of a pyramid, or church steeple. Their coat was probably buttoned up and a slight frown or scowl played across their face. You received very little eye contact.

As you progressed, enthusing about your proposal, you noticed a series of changes taking place. The other person seemed visibly to relax. Perhaps it all started when their ankles were uncrossed and their knees drew upward. The steepled fingers went down onto the desk or onto the tops of their thighs. Their head came up and for the first time they really looked at you.

These changes in body language can be very significant and are strong signals that they are becoming more prepared to listen and even say 'Yes' to your proposition. Of course it can just as easily go the other way. Their body language was quite open and positive at the beginning but gradually closed and became less responsive and negative. Although you do not need to be a body language expert to spot these changes it is quite amazing how many so-called professional salespeople breeze through their day blissfully unaware of any language other than words. And yet body language is far more accurate and significant than the spoken language. Body language analysis is the art of seeing what others are thinking. Because body signals stem from the subconscious, the signals we see are often a more accurate indicator of feelings and thoughts than carefully chosen words.

Verbal signals

Verbal signals which suggest that people are ready to say 'Yes' are likely to be more direct than the non-verbal. Because the words we use can be vague or ambiguous it is not always easy to detect the right moment to go for a decision. Be aware of the pace of their conversation with you. If it slows or speeds up it can indicate a readiness to conclude. Some people prefer to listen long and hard before reaching a conclusion. In this case the situation may reverse and you suddenly find yourself receiving lots of questions.

Here are some examples of ways in which others typically signal that they may be ready to go ahead:

- 'So how soon can you start the project?'
- 'What's the bottom line? How much is this going to cost us, all told?'
- 'Just go through the implementation schedule once more for me.'
- 'Would you be overseeing the project yourself?'
- 'Suppose we want to change things halfway through, would we be able to?'
- 'Can you guarantee the security of your system?'
- 'Could you re-design it to include some important extras?'

The test close

Although these statements or questions do not explicitly accept your proposals the last four do contain a number of presumptions and it would be safe to nudge the questioner towards a decision. This is easier than you might think. The final four questions require an answer and it is important to think about the way in which you construct your reply. For example, you could simply say 'Yes' to all of these questions: 'Yes, we can re-design it'; 'Yes, I will be overseeing the project', and so on.

In future whenever you receive a leading question from the other person answer it like this: 'Would you like us to re-design it?', 'Is it important to you that I oversee the project?', 'Do you think you may want to make changes part-way through?' This is what the salesperson calls a test close. While it does not get you to a final decision it does reveal how others are thinking, how serious their questions are. Here are some more ways in which you could obtain a decision:

The direct decision question

It should be so easy to simply ask the direct question 'Do you agree? Shall we go ahead right away?' yet it is often avoided or left to the very end when more subtle approaches have failed. Its very directness can appeal to the proactive-leader and creative-talker type of character (outlined in Chapter 7). It could take the form:

'OK, Mr Topdog—shall we go ahead?'
'Fine, Mr Jolly. If there are no more questions I propose that we start on Monday.'
'Will you marry me?'

The reason that many people avoid this decision question is because it is a closed question. We have been taught not to ask a closed question. Suppose they say 'No'? We anticipate an impending sense of rejection and avoid the question altogether. Nothing could be more dangerous at this stage of influencing. This is a critical moment, it is easy for people to lose their enthusiasm. If you receive a 'No' then you can always ask (SuperQuestion) 'What's preventing you from going ahead?' and quickly elicit the preventive cause.

The alternative choice decision question

The second approach is less direct because you enable people to make a choice between two possible options:

'When would you like to start? Friday or shall we wait until Monday?'
'Which approach do you prefer?'
'Which film shall we go to see—this one or that one?'
'Would you like tea or do you prefer coffee?'
'Your place or mine?'

The subtlety of this question lies in the fact that you are not asking for a direct decision, only for people to make their minds up about an apparent choice which needs to be made. At the very least they cannot reply with a 'No'.

The minor decision question

Another soft tactic. With this question you are asking people to make a decision concerning a relatively unimportant aspect of your plan. If they reply positively then the assumption is that they will agree to everything else you suggest.

'Oh, by the way, where would you like the logo to appear? At the top of the form or do you feel it would look better bottom right?'
'There is one other thing I meant to ask you. How do you plan to fund the project?'
'How do you think we should inform the northern branches?'
'Do you think we should invite your Auntie Maud to the wedding?'

The assumptive decision question

This question is assumptive and implies that the other person has already agreed to go ahead. Be careful with this tactic. Mr or Ms Analytical-Listener does not like presumption and they will not be afraid to point this out in unequivocal terms. But the assumptive question does work well with the creative-talker or reactive-follower types, both of whom need continuous nudges towards a final decision.

'After we start I assume you will want a monthly report on our progress?'
'When we start the project you will notice significant improvements within the first week or so.'
'Which restaurant shall we go to this weekend?'

The benefit summary

This works well with people who find it difficult to say yes without a great amount of thought. They are probably on the brink of saying 'I'd like to give it some more thought before saying a final "Yes" to the idea'. You can pre-empt this by giving a brief summary of the benefits they will gain. When you do this be sure to remind them of their needs in order to reinforce the connection between needs and benefits.

> Before we conclude the meeting I'd like to sum up what we have discussed. I think we all agreed that your main requirements are security and an accurate record of incidents. Am I right? Good. When you install the new system it will be impossible for any clients to log straight into the system. Only you and your team will have passwords and these will be regularly changed. The client will have to come through your help desk. This in turn will mean that you will be able to log all calls and match them against your Service Level Agreements. Assuming you are happy with this solution I suggest that we begin the installation at the end of this month. Is that a good time for you?

It is a long-winded way of getting to 'Yes' but worth the effort if you want to be sure that you have covered the ground properly. With inveterate analytical-listeners it would be a shrewd move to follow up your benefit summary in writing so that they can mull over your proposal at leisure. Written summaries are useful, too, if your proposals are to be shown to other people. The prime decision maker may well have others on whose suggestions or agreement he/she relies. By putting it all in writing you will be able to answer any questions which may arise and need answering in your absence. In other words—don't rely on other people to sell your ideas down the line. They may attempt to do this but are unlikely to make as thorough a job of it as you could.

The similar situation

How often have you been on the brink of saying yes to a good idea but baulked at the last minute? You may not be the dithery type but it is perfectly normal to harbour last-minute feelings of doubt or concern about an idea. This is particularly true if you are one of the first people to try the idea out. It is natural to want to leave things for a while, to let others be the guinea pigs, and to allow time to iron out any kinks or get rid of unseen bugs.

As the influencer you may find all this very frustrating. You have done your job, identified needs, stressed relevant benefits and dealt with all the objections you received. Now it is decision time and this person still doesn't seem prepared to go ahead. What next? It is time to use your empathy. Put yourself in their shoes and ask yourself: 'If I felt as they do what would help me make a decision? What would I like to hear which would relieve any last-minute doubts and anxieties?'

Tell them about others who have had similar thoughts. Talk them through the sequence of events which led to a final decision. Reassure them that all the doubts and fears vanished after the other person had made the final decision. Tell them how happy this person is with their decision, how they cannot think why they left it so long before making a change. If it is practical you could put them in touch with others who have made similar decisions. Recall how effective testimonials are when you see them in advertisements. These often contrast a 'before' with a favourable 'after' allowing you to put yourself in others' shoes, to tread the path they have so successfully taken.

After the decision has been taken—what next?

Having gained agreement, it would be very easy and potentially fatal to assume that you need do nothing more than rest on your laurels, congratulating yourself on a job well done. After all they have agreed to your proposition, implementation is under way and at this stage nothing can be lost.

Think again. How often have you suffered from so-called 'buyer's remorse'? You have made a decision to buy something. You are convinced of your needs, you can afford it and what's more—you want it. But mysteriously by the time you reach home you have some serious doubts about your decision. Perhaps you don't really need it. Maybe it was a frivolous decision—you merely want it. Anyway it cost a lot—more than you could really afford at this time. What will your partner, colleagues, friends say when you tell them about it?

It is perfectly normal to go through a post-decision depression. As a professional influencer you will want to put some strategies in place for reassuring people that they did after all make the right decision.

Exercise—Keeping them convinced of the merits of your proposal

1. Imagine that you have successfully convinced a colleague to agree to a simple job share—you do some of her work and she does some of yours. The benefits are straightforward. You will both have more variety within your jobs, you will be able to cover for one another in times of absence. But benefits alone will not necessarily sustain their faith in the idea. Benefits can wear thin after a while.

2. What will you do or say which will keep your colleague happy and content that she did do the right thing after all?

   What will help reinforce her decision
   - On a practical level?
   - On an emotional level?
   - On a psychological level?

Summary

1. By understanding why you avoid making decisions you can begin to understand why others avoid them.
2. Understanding your preferred decision-making criteria can throw valuable light on the habits and conventions

of others. Also, it may indicate limitations in the way you choose to elicit decisions from other people.

3. Watch for the signals, verbal and non-verbal, which will tell you when the time has come to ask for a decision.
4. Cultivate a wide range of methods, techniques or strategies in order to get positive agreement.
5. Your involvement will not necessarily cease once a decision has been reached. Your support may be needed in order to reassure anyone suffering from post-decision depression syndrome!

Chapter 11

Influencing groups

It takes three weeks to deliver a good ad lib speech.
Mark Twain

There comes a time in most professional careers when someone says, 'Will you present your findings to the weekly meeting' or 'We have been asked to present a paper at the annual conference. As you have been closely involved I think you are the person to handle it for us'. This chapter explores some less conventional ways of influencing a group presentation or meeting.

Unfair as it may sound, people in business and social life are often measured by their ability to talk in public. It doesn't seem to matter that you are an expert or have important or useful information about a subject—it is vital that you present it well. The way in which you present and the consequent effectiveness of your influence with the group is critical. Unfair, yes—but critical even so. Of course, knowing this does nothing to calm our state of mind when we are invited to give the talk. In fact it usually exacerbates the situation. Most of us feel our stomach looping the loop, our palms running with perspiration and our mouth drying at the mere thought of having to do it. Recent research suggests that there are three common fears which haunt us:

1. speaking to groups
2. heights
3. spiders.

If you are ever invited to speak to airline passengers on the subject of tarantulas I suggest you decline gracefully. But why is the thought of public speaking such universal anathema? After all, we have probably been asked to give a talk because we are seen as an expert, someone who has been part of a project and understands it thoroughly, someone who is enthusiastic and knowledgeable, someone who can represent the company/group/department. A large part of the fear we experience can be due to anticipation. We are worried that someone in the audience will know more than we do. We are concerned that we may forget something vital or, worse still, dry up altogether. We are frightened at the prospect of being in the spotlight with all eyes focused on us.

Three ways to minimize fears

There are three ways in which you can begin to overcome your fears and phobias. Notice that I have used the word 'minimize'. It is unlikely that the fear of anticipation will ever leave you entirely. It could be argued that a certain amount of trepidation is desirable. After all it does suggest that we are concerned about the outcome, that we want things to go well. Even the most hardened of professionals feel distinct twinges of adrenaline as they rise to their feet. Ask any of them how they feel about this and they will tell you that they use adrenaline to 'fly'. It provides a fuel to lift them off at the beginning of their talk. And they will also tell you that it dies down and becomes controllable after a couple of minutes or so.

Here then are the three ways you can minimize any fears you may have:

- Prepare and structure your talk before you deliver it. (You would be amazed at the number of people who tell me that they make it all up as they go along. Or who say that they don't want to be tied down to anything too rigidly.)
- Rehearse, rehearse, rehearse. Leave nothing to chance. Enlist the help of a group of colleagues or friends, sit them down and make them listen to your presentation. Ask for questions, comments, criticism. Prime them to ask you the most difficult questions. Even ask them to be rowdy or uninterested if these are audience reactions you expect.
- Recognize that you will always feel the fear. Be aware that practically everyone who rises to their feet in front of an audience feels it too. Notice how it slowly fades away as time ticks by. Discover that most of the feelings you have are inside your body and mind. No-one can actually see them.

One of the most consistent comments I hear when I run presentation training sessions is: 'Hey, I look a lot better on the video tape than I did when I was delivering the talk. I don't appear anywhere near as nervous as I felt as I was delivering it.'

Fear is very often a: **F**alse **E**xpectation **A**bout **R**eality.

Planning and preparing to influence groups

Like many things in life, time and effort spent in the planning and preparation phase can be the most valuable investment you will make. Here are some pointers:

- Use your influencing checklist (Chapter 1).
- Ask yourself 'What precisely do I want the group to know, understand or agree to?'

- Because people only listen with 25% efficiency limit yourself to *three key messages.*
- Who is the main decision maker? Will any subsidiary decision makers be present?
- How much do they know about the subject?
- What are their needs, requirements, wants?
- Will my ideas fulfil those needs? Can I prove it?
- Can I justify any direct or indirect costs?
- What resistance can I expect? From whom? How will I handle it?
- What approach will suit the group (input from me; questions and answers; detailed handouts; plenty of pictures; statistics; drama; emotion)?
- What style of influence should I use (autocratic; democratic; logical; emotional; assertive; passive; persuasive; negotiation)?
- How do I plan to gain commitment?

Mind mapping

There are many proven ways of structuring a formal presentation. One of the most common is the so-called mind map. The underlying strength of the formal presentation is that it allows you the presenter an opportunity to influence a group of people. If their brains are to relate to your information and be influenced by you the content of your presentation must be organized so as to fit in, as elegantly as possible, to their way of thinking. In his book *Use Your Head* Tony Buzan says: 'It follows that if the brain works with Key concepts in an interlinked and integrated manner, our notes and our world relations should in many instances be structured in this way rather than in traditional lines. Rather than starting from the top and working down in sentences or lists, one should start from the centre with the main idea and branch out as dictated by the individual ideas and general form of the central theme.'

Mind maps have several advantages over the linear form of note taking:

- The bulk of notes is significantly reduced.
- Your central idea is more clearly defined.
- The words you choose will be richer in imagery.
- The process of choosing these words requires you to have a greater understanding of your material.
- Associating words with ideas will help you recall the key points more readily.
- The more significant ideas and subheadings will be closer to the centre.
- Less important ideas will be nearer the edge.
- The ways in which apparently separate ideas link together will become obvious as the map progresses. This will allow you to make changes in structure quite early on in the map's development.
- Any new ideas can easily be added without altering the general flow.
- Each mind map you create will be unique. This will aid recall and re-use or further development of subsequent presentations.
- Because it allows you to note your ideas in a random fashion the open-ended structure will help your brain to identify new connections more easily.

This is a very practical tool for seeing how your ideas fit together and will provide a simple way of shaping a well-defined structure. It may also provide useful insight into what material you could leave out altogether.

Example of a mind map

Let us suppose that you have been invited to choose a new computer system for your company. You have analysed the needs of key individuals and departments and researched the market. You have noted possible anxieties and doubts and have developed counter-arguments. A simple mind map would look something like this:

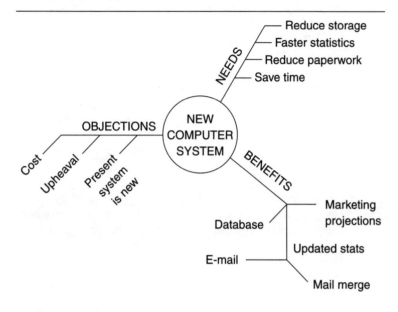

Figure 11.1   Linear format for structuring a presentation

Now you have completed your mind map and can see the wood for the trees here is an example of a more detailed format for convincing a group to agree to an idea or proposition.

1. *State your objective*
   'I aim to help you choose the most suitable system.'
2. *Re-cap and agree principal needs*
   - To reduce flow of paperwork between departments and remote offices.
   - To provide fast statistical breakdowns.
   - To use information in order to reduce unnecessary storage of finished products.
3. *List three main benefits of your proposed recommendation*
   - Instant and accurate projections of market requirements will let you know precisely when products will be needed.

- Simple-to-use formulae and macros will provide continuously updated statistics.
- Electronic mail and voice mail will reduce letters and memos within the company.

4. *Outframe any possible objections*
- Accept that there may be valid objections to your suggestion and meet them head on.
- Answer these in turn and obtain agreement that your answers have been accepted.
- Support your solutions to problems and resistance with re-affirmations of your three main benefits.
- If you cannot answer any objections work hard to minimize their impact on your proposals. Make sure you gain agreement before moving on to:

5. *Outline 'where we go from here'*
- Arrange site visits to similar organizations who already use the system.
- Arrange for your IT people to undergo immersion training in hardware and software usage.
- Set up meetings with the computer company system analysts.
- Dry-run the system prior to installation.
- Negotiate system service agreements.
- Agree a provisional install date.
- Meet and form relationships with the computer product installation team.

This more formal listing of content now allows you to create your notes. These can range from simple cue cards to larger A5 or even A4 sheets. Most conference presenters like to write everything down as in a speech, highlighting key messages. Others who use overhead projectors simply jot a few pointers on the edge of the view foil cardboard frame! Each to his own. The key to it all is understanding what strategy works best for you—and sticking to it.

Establishing rapport

Establishing rapport is arguably the single most important skill needed when influencing others. Influence is sharing information or experience between or among individuals with the aim of bringing about, or avoiding, change. Usually resistance or barriers to your influence will be present in some form. A sense of mutual rapport between you, the presenter, and your audience will help eliminate many barriers or perceived differences. Having good rapport with your audience will:

1. Help you to establish and maintain control by staying in constant tune with the prevailing situation, to align with whatever is happening and to imperceptibly help others change direction or views.
2. Help you establish credibility and trust with your audience. Without these you will find it difficult to overcome hostility, anger and resistance to change.
3. Help others to understand you more clearly. By getting in step with and understanding how they understand and interpret their 'reality' you will be able to present your ideas in ways which make good sense to them.

Rapport with individuals and key players within the group

Good rapport with key players within the group is at least as important as having rapport with the group as a whole. It is highly likely that these key figures will have considerable long-term and overriding influence on the thought patterns and ultimate decisions reached by the group itself. A typical group in a company might contain an interlocking set of individuals. Each individual may have separate thoughts, needs and motives but these could overlap (or even conflict with) others in the team.

Take a typical management structure with individuals who have apparently mutual goals. On closer examination you may find that these goals and aims in fact conflict in some way. This is because they are seen from a different perspective.

Suppose you are planning a presentation where you aim to persuade colleagues to invest in a new product. You have an audience of around eight or ten which includes the following:

Managing Director Entrepreneurial drive for aggressive acquisition of market share and short-term profit growth. Wants to have things agreed quickly and without fuss. Could say 'Yes' on the spot.

Financial Accountant Has concern for capital investment and the cost of borrowing. Wants to see solid proof and evidence of long-term investment potential. Unlikely to agree without more detail and further meetings.

Production Controller Pleased to be able to take up available production capacity. Eager to begin.

Sales Manager Recognizes the need to take on more salespeople. Concerned with short-term sales/cost ratio. Doubtful of ultimate value of your proposal.

Clearly, it would not be difficult to convince the MD and the Production Controller. But if you did convince them you would be up against the other two, both of whom have strong reasons for not wanting to go ahead. You may be lucky and the Managing Director might simply line up with Production and railroad the decision through in favour of your ideas. Formal authority wins the day. But equally strongly, dissatisfaction might set in. The Accountant and the Sales Manager, feeling aggrieved that their protestations have been ignored, may well work covertly to sabotage the final outcome. And they are well placed to do this.

This is where your rapport skills come in. Using your empathy, putting yourself in the shoes of all four individuals, you will start to see things as they do. Early rapport with the Financial Accountant and Sales Manager will incorporate their concerns and will alleviate some of these early on in the presentation.

A simple checklist of ways to gain/maintain rapport with different people in the group might contain some of the

following (this list is not exhaustive as different circumstances and group mixes will demand different approaches).

- Shake hands with as many people as time or size of
  group allows.
- Acknowledge them by name, title or discipline whenever appropriate.
- Establish early eye contact with key players and secondary influencers.
- Mention the title or worth of their job function as
  often as possible.
- Reaffirm their personal needs throughout the presentation.
- Acknowledge their possible doubts and fears and
  reassure them that you understand them.

Rapport with the whole group

As groups are dynamic, moods and attitudes can swing quite
rapidly from positive to negative, or vice versa. As a presenter your antennae must be constantly quivering, watching
out for those subtle and not so subtle changes which could
signal important shifts in the outlook of the group.

- Watch people's body language. Notice significant
  changes.
- When changes occur, do something different. Speed
  up—slow down. Sit down, ask for questions. Suggest
  a short comfort break. Talk louder, faster, slower.
  Break off and recount a (pertinent) anecdote. Invite
  relevant experiences which confirm your main
  message.
- Let the group know that you recognize the part they
  play in a corporate identity: 'As residents of Willow
  Park Estate you will all know only too well . . .'

Future pacing

Future pacing is a technique which allows the audience to imagine a situation in the future where the knowledge they are gaining from your presentation will be useful.

One way to achieve this is to allow your audience to *visualize* a future situation unfolding and to *imagine* their new skills or knowledge being used successfully. Another approach is to extend the imagined situation by asking your audience to imagine how they will *feel* when they have achieved something, or to *hear* other people congratulating them on their achievement.

Pre-supposition

Pre-supposition uses words and phrases which pre-suppose that some thing or event will take place in the future.

- 'When you return to your office and find yourself using this information . . .'
- 'You will discover that these ideas will be . . .'
- 'Shall we break now or in fifteen minutes?'

Embedded commands

Embedded commands are messages woven into other messages which have a specific and intended outcome. It is possible to command your audience to do something you want: 'Although I will be giving handouts at the end of my presentation you may like to . . . *take notes as we go . . .* which will supplement my handout material.'

A more oblique use of the embedded command is: 'When you use these ideas *successfully* in your work . . .' 'Although you feel that . . . *I have covered everything . . .* there may be a *couple of quick questions . . .* some of you would like to ask before we . . . *go into lunch.*'

Analogy

Analogy is one of the most useful communication tools. It can help your audience grasp something in 10 seconds which may ordinarily take them 60 or 90 seconds to understand. It's as easy as ABC to use. 'The form is very similar to the car tax document.' 'The software is rather like a basic word processing package . . .'

Metaphor, parables, anecdotes and reference experiences

Since time began people have told stories to one another. In all parts of the world the story still has enormous significance in helping us to form a view of life. Too many presentations and meetings are dry and laboured. Audiences often crave a little excitement, fun or emotion. At first sight this may seem out of place in the context of a formal meeting or presentation. But how often have you noticed how effective laughter can be as an ice-breaker? People instantly relax and seem somehow more compliant and open to suggestion.

Metaphor is an elegant way of telling a story which contains a hidden message. In Gregory Bateson's book, *Steps to an Ecology of Mind*, he tells about a man who wanted to know about the mind. What was it? Would computers ever be as intelligent as humans? The man entered the following question into the world's most powerful computer: 'Do you compute that you will ever think like a human being?'

The computer coughed and spluttered, rumbled, went quiet for a long time then printed out its reply. The man tore it out of the printer in great excitement and read the following words: 'That reminds me of a story . . .'

Metaphors are used widely in therapy. This is because the client who is undergoing therapy may feel that that they have a firm grip on reality. Talking to them in their own language will generally result in circular and repetitive dialogue, using the same language patterns and descriptive terms. (Have you ever noticed how domestic arguments often follow an almost ritualistic pattern, from the first

words through to the inevitable conclusion?) Therapists
have found that one neat and simple way to *apparently* talk
about the client's 'reality' is to use metaphor, stories, jokes,
parables, experiences or other examples. This allows the
therapist to make small but significant changes in the way
the story is told. By doing this he or she changes its perspective and the perspective of the client. Once this has taken
place it is often a simple matter to reframe the background
and causes of the problem and thus its potential for
change and eventual resolution.

On a more basic level metaphor can sound something
like: 'I recall how difficult it was as a child to learn tables.
It seemed completely impossible. But slowly I started to put
them into my unconscious mind so that now when someone
says "four sevens" I don't need to *think* of the answer—it
just comes.' Followed by: ' ... so even if you find some of
my material a little difficult to understand now, *in the future*
when you are *using it successfully*, you will discover that it
comes naturally from your unconscious mind.' (Note the
added pre-supposition and embedded command in the last
sentence.)

Anchoring parts of the room

An anchor is any powerful stimulus–response mechanism.
For example, some people feel hungry just by walking into
their kitchen. You can use this powerful tool in your presentations to increase understanding, acceptance and empathy
with your audience.

As a presenter you wear many hats—for example, you
may be casual, friendly, chatty. Some of the time you may
want to be particularly dramatic, or serious. Then again, you
may want to make explicit suggestions or orders to the
audience. Some of the time you will be presenting cold
facts—other times you will want to interact with the audience or make an announcement.

When you are being particularly serious, for example, you
will speak in a different tone and pace your message in a
special way. You could also go to another part of the room

to speak from, thus *anchoring* the spot to what you are saying. Throughout your presentation, whenever you want to place special emphasis on a message you can move back to the same place in the room, pause and make your points. Subconsciously, your audience will understand the significance of this ritual as it happens and will be far more susceptible to suggestions made from that part of the room.

(A typical example of this is the speaker who sits quite casually on the front edge of the desk to make general administrative announcements but then moves behind the desk, stands and speaks louder when starting the presentation proper.)

Gaining group agreement

There were two prime reasons why you convened this group to hear your ideas:

1. To influence them to do something.
2. To persuade them to agree to do it.

The route to agreement can be fraught with danger and frustration. You think you have convinced them when someone at the back asks: 'Have you thought about the Northern Division? How will they feel about your idea?' Your audience looks at one another and nods significantly. A murmur rises, becomes a babble and you realize that you have lost your grip. You have been heading down one route and the guy at the back has been on an entirely different path.

When you commute to a well-known destination you will have some alternative routes in mind. This is in case there are unforeseen delays or hold-ups. You check the map and memorize possible alternatives. It is the same when you present. You have a destination (group agreement with your ideas) and similarly you will need to have several possible routes to success.

Use SuperQuestions

When a participant at your meeting or presentation says 'We cannot do that' ask: 'What exactly is it that prevents you from doing it?' Do not ask 'Why?', simply seek the apparent preventive cause.

Risk is about breaking from the past. It is possible that you are asking the group to make a risk calculation or assessment. Many in the group will want to maintain the status quo, preferring the known to the scary unknown. A useful SuperQuestion to ask your audience is: 'What will happen if we don't change?' What will be the consequences of inactivity? How will this affect our standing in a competitive marketplace? In what ways will risks taken be counterbalanced by benefits gained?

Question carefully the motives of people who seem to take delight in scuppering your plans at the last minute. Why didn't they introduce their doubts earlier on? Why have they waited until the end before trying to sink your proposal? If it seems appropriate ask the rest of the group or audience: 'How do you feel about John's thoughts? Does he have a point?' A quick head count will reveal the strength of feeling within the group. It is often the case that those who introduce last-minute doubts are unsure of benefits of your proposal or simply flexing their muscles in front of peers or superiors. But be careful. You may win this argument but unless it is handled carefully you may find that the boat-rocker manages to reverse the situation on a later occasion.

Summary

1. Minimize fear through detailed preparation, rehearsal and the awareness that stage fright can become a fuel which propels your performance to great heights.
2. Time spent in planning your performance can be the most valuable investment you will make.
3. Structure your session around three basic points. Use a

mind map to help you identify these and to notice how you can link common information.

4. Work hard to establish rapport with the group itself as well as individuals and key players.

5. Use future pacing, pre-supposition and embedded commands to reinforce your message.

6. Use analogy, metaphor, anecdotes, stories, reference experiences, even jokes to bring life and style to your performance.

7. Use power words to add weight to your message.

Chapter 12

Influencing on the telephone

Don't call me. I'll call you

With so many of us owning a telephone and with so few of us receiving any formal training in its use it is easy to understand why this special means of communication can be badly handled. We can't live without it but perversely the telephone can become our worst enemy. This chapter looks at ways of overcoming telephone prejudices, helping you to get the best from one of today's most frequently used forms of communication.

It has been said that human beings spend 80% of their waking hours communicating with others. Thirty per cent of this time is devoted to talking while 45% is listening. And yet it is estimated that within one hour of holding a conversation over half of what we just heard is forgotten or at best open to gross misinterpretation. There are four key causes of potential communication problems when we use the telephone:

1. We have no visual clues.
2. We can lose control of the conversation.
3. Telephone conversations are expected to be brief.

4.   The telephone is widely regarded as an intrusion.

Lack of visual clues

In some respects the fact that we cannot see the person we are talking to on the telephone can be an advantage. When we talk face to face our senses are bombarded with information. We see so many things which are unconnected with the conversation subject matter. Another person walks by, a door opens and closes, a bus parks outside the window. Not serious distractions perhaps but distractions even so. In some respects therefore, by isolating the words people say, the telephone has a singular advantage over other means of influence.

However, when we persuade someone to make a decision we support our proposition with appropriate benefits. Without access to that person, without seeing them in their surroundings, it can be difficult to relate benefits directly to their circumstances or value and belief system. When we make a point, how do we know for certain that the other person agrees with it? The subtle non-verbal clues which accompany all our communications with the world are simply not there. So when the other person says 'Yes' how can we be sure that they don't mean 'Maybe' or even 'No'?

Over the last decade a great deal of attention has been paid to 'relationships'. 'Ours is a people business'; 'The customer is King'; 'Customer satisfaction is everything.' The emphasis is no longer on what we influence others to do but on how well we are able to relate to others. It is essential that the telephone environment which we create is structured by the values, beliefs, needs and wants of the other person. There is a strong case to be made for several short telephone calls rather than one long one. Taking time to become acquainted with the other person (or if we already know them, to reinforce the relationship) can pay handsome dividends. In 1979 US investment brokers Merrill Lynch did a study and found that the prime reason why a customer chose a broker was that they liked the person they were dealing with. Honesty and trust came second and third. Lastly was the ability to make money.

Before you pick up the telephone to convince someone ask yourself this question:

> Which is most important to me—to convince the other person or to persuade them to agree with me?

There is a subtle difference. To wish to convince the other person means that you are focused on the content of your message, on your outcome rather than theirs. To persuade them to agree with your ideas means that you are focusing on them the person, on their needs, fears, aspirations.

Using your voice to develop rapport on the telephone

Telephone communication can be summed up as 'What you say and how you say it'. When we think of 'the voice' we tend to restrict our thoughts to voice tone. When striving to gain rapport there is much more to be achieved through our voices than simply tone:

- We can adjust the rate at which we speak.
- We can control the volume at which we speak.
- We can choose the words we use when we speak.

Before looking at these three important variables let's examine the importance of voice tone. Earlier on in this book I quoted research into the channels through which we perceive one another. Voice tone contributes a colossal 38% to the total message we present. The emphasis we choose to place on each and every word we say can radically alter the perceived meaning of our communication. Take a simple statement—'I would like you to have the report ready for Friday's meeting'. In how many ways can we alter the meaning or shift the emphasis of this simple sentence?

'*I* would like you to have the report ready for Friday's meeting.'
'I *would* like you to have the report ready for Friday's meeting.'
'I would *like* you to have the report ready for Friday's meeting.'
'I would like *you* to have the report ready for Friday's meeting.'
'I would like you to have *the report* ready for Friday's meeting.'
'I would like you to have the report *ready* for Friday's meeting.'
'I would like you to have the report ready for *Friday's* meeting.'
'I would like you to have the report ready for Friday's *meeting.*'

One statement—eight tonal variants giving eight substantially different emphases of meaning and intent. How often have you heard the words 'very urgent' and been able to tell precisely *how* urgent by registering the emphasis placed on 'very' or 'urgent'?

Controlling your rate of speech

There are fast speakers and slow speakers. The fast speakers tend to think that the slow speakers are irritatingly hesitant, fumbling for words and putting the listener way ahead of the conversation. On the other hand the slow speakers simply cannot cope with the torrent of words coming down the line. Which are you—fast or slow? Do you adjust your rate of speech to match precisely that of the person you are trying to influence? It is so easy to do, yet so easy to overlook. This is a subtle and effective way of matching and gaining early rapport with a person you may never have met and certainly cannot see. Even if the other person is verging on the hysterical, gabbling their sentences and falling over their words it is still perfectly possible to match them in volume and speed, then imperceptibly to slow down the rate and reduce the volume until you are speaking quite levelly and normally noticing at the same time how your control of your state has affected theirs.

Controlling the volume of your voice

For many people the volume at which they speak is used to signal their mood. At a time of sadness or mourning it is normal and socially appropriate to speak quietly. On the other hand this approach would appear unusual at a party or large social gathering. Some people become quiet and speak with a calm regularity when they are angry or displeased. Others let rip and shout. As you begin to notice the different ways in which others conduct themselves, how they use their voice volume as a platform to support messages or moods, notice too how this affects you. Are you intimidated by those who shout or talk loudly? Do people who speak quietly and calmly only succeed in irritating you?

Matching volume of speech can be a slightly scary thing to try if you have not done it before. At first glance it seems counter-productive to yell back at someone who is blasting off at you. But put yourself in their shoes for a moment. How might they feel if you remain cool and calm? They would rightly think that there is a mismatch just as they would if they were happy and positive when you were the opposite.

Why match speech at all? Why is it so important? Because it is a prelude to leading the other person to where you want them to go. People who speak loudly and forcefully can be led quickly towards a quieter and calmer mood. Here's how it might sound.

Them: (loudly) 'I do not agree with you and that is final.'
You: (same volume) 'Yes, and I can see your point of view.' (slightly quieter) 'What we need to do is find out where the differences lie and sort things out.' (even quieter) 'I am sure that you will agree that we can both gain if we can settle these minor points.'

Them: (far quieter) 'Well, yes, I suppose you're right. So—what exactly do you propose?'

Of course in real life this dialogue may well last longer. If you fail to match and lead go back to the original volume and do it again. Persist and you will eventually succeed.

Matching words and speech patterns

Matching words and speech patterns is simple but subtle. As an experiment listen to professional radio presenters. With only one sensory channel, hearing, through which to express themselves they usually speak economically and expressively. Listen for a few minutes then mimic the presenter. Notice how different this is from how you would normally say the same thing.

We humans see the world from our own singular viewpoint. We spend large portions of our day describing to others this 'reality' as we see it. As our 'reality' is only a personal perception it is often difficult and even counterproductive to attempt to alter it. To step inside other people's 'reality' requires that we use their methods of describing it. For instance they may use adjectives such as beautiful, large, nice. Or adverbs like quickly, easily, approximately. Close analysis of these six words reveals nothing. What do they mean, exactly? What is 'nice'? How approximate is 'approximately'?

Unless you need to know the precise meaning of these descriptive words do not bother to use a SuperQuestion—simply use the same word in your response:

Them: 'We want to get this done quickly.'
You: 'So doing it quickly is important to you?'

The use of so-called speech patterns is very similar. Many of us have pet phrases which we use frequently. We know what we mean when we use these words. Here are some examples:

'Know what I mean?'
'I hear what you say.'
'Yep. Okay. Got it.'
'Right. Sure. Fine.'

There is often a link between preferred speech patterns and personality. For instance, the proactive, impulsive dominant extrovert type may use 'Yep, okay, got it' to suggest a quick mind, or a need to move on. The strong silent dominant introvert may say: 'Hhmm yes, I believe I know what you mean and fully concur with your point of view.' The jolly submissive extrovert often uses phrases such as: 'I'm pretty pleased to hear that. Great, let's talk more.' The cautious submissive introvert on the other hand will be less outgoing, less garrulous: 'Er, I'm a bit unsure of that last point. Would you mind very much just going over it once more. Sorry.'

Listen and match whenever it is appropriate. You do not have to copy slavishly, merely echo what you hear. People like people who are like themselves.

Telephone words to use

Short words used within short sentences suggest direct action. Long rambling phrases full of subordinate clauses merely generate confusion, if you get my meaning, I mean most of us do it from time to time, well maybe not most but certainly lots do, I expect you've seen that haven't you, it's all too common these days, and it's really easy to lose your way within a conversation if you're not very careful.

I hope the point is made. Most adults experience increasing difficulty in following the sense of a spoken sentence of more than 18 words.

Using names on the telephone

It is becoming more common in the Western world to talk on first-name terms with people we have never met. The Microsoft Corporation recently experimented with a new telephone sales service in the United Kingdom. Their operators greeted callers by saying: 'Good morning, thank you for calling Microsoft Connection, you're through to Darren, how may I help?' Analysis showed that on average over 40% of callers immediately replied using their own first name: 'Good morning, my name is Richard Storey and I was wondering if . . .' 'Thank you for calling, Richard. If I can be of further help you can reach me on extension 4951—just ask for Darren.'

Some love this approach, others hate it. The trick is to gauge correctly by listening to the way the other person chooses to introduce themselves. Then match it. It is useful to refer to others by name at the beginning of the conversation, maybe once or twice during it and definitely at the end. But do not fall into the trap of overusing names of people you do not know on the telephone. After a while it becomes obvious and counter-productive.

Summary

1.   Use your voice to develop rapport on the phone.
2.   Control your rate of speech.
3.   Be aware of the volume of your voice.
4.   Match the other person's words and speech patterns.
5.   Use the other person's name—but don't overuse it.

Chapter 13

Writing to win

The pen is mightier than the sword. E.G. Bulwer-Lytton

The need to influence others in writing is common to virtually every public and private sector business. Every day businesses throughout the world generate millions of letters, faxes, reports and proposals. This chapter explores ways in which some of today's advertising copywriters and the composers of successful sales letters use influence in print.

Although English is the most common business language in use, different applications, spelling and usage create an immense potential for international misunderstanding. The population of the United States makes up the largest national group of English-speakers, outnumbering all the rest of the native English-speakers of the world. Waves of British immigrants took English to Africa, Australia, New Zealand and other parts of what was known as the British Empire. Written English in these countries (including India, Hong Kong, Malaysia, Jamaica, Belize and Bermuda) has generally maintained conventional British usage.

If your document is to be seen in another country make quite sure that as far as possible it conforms to the expectations of the local reader. Nothing is more likely to develop resistance in your reader than ignorance of local convention.

Eight steps towards more convincing reports and proposals

1. Shake hands with your readers. Always incorporate a covering letter (or memo if the report is for internal consumption).
2. Emphasize your credentials.
3. As far as possible within the constraints laid down in the terms of reference, write in your own style.
4. Length proves nothing. There are no rules which state how long a manuscript should be. It should be as long as is necessary to make your points. But no longer.
5. Although reports and proposals are conventionally written in an impersonal style, e.g. 'It will be appreciated that', 'It has been concluded that', it is better to try to connect with the reader more directly. Try 'As you can see' or 'As engineers you will understand only too well . . .'
6. Put some sell into your report title. 'Improving efficiency through XYZ'.
7. Short reports (twelve pages or less) do not require tables of contents, appendices and so on.
8. Don't overdress the document. Embossed leather with gold tooling may sell a dictionary but your proposal probably needs only a simple line drawing.

Style

Style is usually dictated by the internal approach adopted by the organization you work in, or to whom you are writing. Solicited proposals often demand that quite strict conventions of layout, style and content are to be followed to the letter. This approach, while easy to conform to, allows little or no opportunity for individuality in writing style.

As a general rule style should conform to the A, B, C of written English:

A—Accuracy
B—Brevity
C—Clarity

Accuracy is clearly a vital component of written material. If in conversation you say something that is inaccurate others will point out the error, or you will quickly correct yourself. Once you have written inaccuracies it is impossible to redeem the situation. It is there for all to see for evermore—in writing, with your name at the bottom. Check, double-check and check once more to remove anything that is wrong, is inconsistent or is a misprint or typo. I once worked for a Managing Director who was an expert at discovering errors in reports. He would open the document at a random page and flick through it. Then he would stop, examine some part of it and look up. You knew what was coming. 'This doesn't seem quite right, does it?' We would hurriedly turn to the offending word or figure. He was usually right and despite our frantic excuses his discovery would mar the impact we had hoped to create.

Brevity is another critical aspect of writing. It is a commonly held belief that the length of a document somehow indicates the amount of time or effort that has been invested in its creation. This may be the case—but the average readers (especially those at the top) do not have the time to plough through fat reports. They want to know what you are recommending, your basic conclusions, the cost, and the implementation schedule. The ways and means of arriving at these are generally of little importance to the busy reader. If your document is more than a few pages long create a short 'executive summary' to accompany the main report. (This will guarantee a high readership for your report as everyone likes to think of themselves as an executive!)

Clarity in writing style involves simplicity and directness. Take these two extracts as an example (both adapted from actual reports):

Example one
Careful consideration has been given by the members of the subcommittee to the question of whether it is in any way necessary or desirable that new legislation should be passed in order to facilitate the transfer of public house licences into newly developed urban neighbourhood areas, so as to follow the consequent movement of populations.

Example two
Traditional centres of pedagogical training were not all taken by surprise by the contemporary socio-economic challenges of the 1990s. The catalogue of changes that have occurred in them during the last decade is an impressive evidence of their ability to make important adjustments required by new situations. To what extent, however, such innovative adjustments have sufficiently replaced older habits or contributed to the sociological reorientation of teacher training is an open question. It may take more time than we think for these adjustments to reveal their total cumulative significance.

In the first extract there are several features that contribute to a lack of clarity:

- The sentence is too long. Keep sentence length at about 18 words.
- There are too many unnecessary words ('Careful consideration has been given by the members of the subcommittee' could easily be reduced to 'The subcommittee considered . . .')
- There is no punctuation to assist the reader.
- The subject ' . . . transfer of public house licences . . .' appears after the object ' . . . new legislation . . .' This is a common problem, known as 'subject–object inversion', and can confuse the reader. A simple sentence comprising noun/verb/object such as 'The cat sat on the mat' can be radically altered if the subject and object are inverted—'The mat was underneath the cat.'

Extract number two also lacks clarity but for different reasons.

- There is an overuse of long words. 'Traditional centres of pedagogical training' could just as easily be called 'Old-style teacher training colleges'.
- Unnecessary adjectives are added to most of the key nouns—'*impressive* evidence', '*important* adjustments', '*sociological* reorientation'. In many cases these could be dropped without affecting the general sense and meaning of the paragraph.
- It has a pompous tone—one teacher writing to impress another?

To check the clarity of your writing you can either show it to a friend or colleague whose opinion and judgement you value or use one of the many grade-level indices contained in word processors. A well-known index which you can easily apply to your own written material is called the fog index (or factor). The word 'fog' in this case refers to clarity of style. Devised in the United States this results in an index which relates to the minimum reading age required to absorb the writing with ease.

Calculating the fog index

To calculate your fog index take a passage of about 100 words (this should contain no quotations). Divide by the number of sentences giving average sentence length (A). Now total the number of words which have three or more syllables (avoiding proper names or nouns and any words which have prefixes or suffixes which increase their length to three syllables, e.g. creat*ed*; amount*ing*; *re*arrange) Call this total (B).

Add totals A and B and multiply by a factor of 0.4 giving the fog index. The final figure approximately represents the minimum reading age required by your reader in order to make immediate sense of your written passage. For instance British newspapers have the following typical fog index range: *The Sun* 6–8; *Daily Express, Daily Mail* 10–12; *Daily Telegraph, Guardian, Times* 14–18; *Independent* 20–24.

Complex material containing technical terms can be made easier to read by reducing the average length of your sentences. If your sentences tend to be made longer by the addition of subordinate clauses (over 18 words) you can reduce the fog index by cutting down polysyllabic words.

You can tell a book by its cover

One of my clients manufacture aircraft instrumentation and are frequently asked to bid for business, usually against competition from Germany and the United States. Although the structure of the proposals themselves is strictly geared to an agreed format the look of the actual covers of the proposals were not specified. For a time my client would design quite lavish covers—glossy full-colour photographs of fighter plane cockpits with head-up displays roaring past mountains of cumulus cloud. Then they had a visit from the Ministry of Defence. They were told to restrict future covers to plain blue with black print.

What does this tell you about the power of presentation? Clearly the MoD were aware that the content of my client's proposals might have become secondary to the *look* of the proposals themselves. However, a flashy proposal will not necessarily win business but a carelessly written bid will definitely contribute to losing the business.

- If your company sells computer equipment use a drawing or photograph of the equipment or a person or people operating it.
- If your product is a service use line drawings or photographs of people performing or receiving your service.
- If your company provides software products an over-printed copy of the output as it applies to the reader would be interesting.

Physical organization

A large part of the process of influencing people in writing is to make things easy for the reader. One client of mine once wrote a lengthy report to his Board and out of a sense of perversity or just plain ignorance decided not to summarize his recommendations. They were there, all right, but scattered throughout the text. This strategy forced his readers to search out his recommendations or even to read the whole text in order to find out what they were (rather like a murder mystery). As the report had taken several months to compile it was a long document and my client asked me to give him feedback, in particular to answer the question:

> After nearly nine months why haven't I had any feedback from the Board?

The answer was simple—he had not attempted to make life easy for his important readers. He imagined that they would rush home clutching his exciting report to their bosoms eager to tuck up in bed early for an engrossing read. Not so. Probably what happened was that the Board members took one look at the report and passed it down the line to some poor assistant for appraisal. In any event the report, its findings and secret recommendations sank without trace.

Your executive summary is a key tool for influencing readers who may not have the time or inclination to read your whole report and should include:

- a concise description of how your proposals address the agreed needs of the reader;
- a brief narrative version of your proposals;
- brief mention of any assumptions which you may have made;
- minimal technical detail;
- little or no unfamiliar technical jargon;
- no detailed pricing information, but an overall cost figure may be appropriate;

- brief details of implementation requirements and timings (only brief as these will be outlined in full elsewhere in your report).

Page layout

Reduce clutter and make your report as readable and visually pleasing as you can. Wide margins, double spacing, indentations, clear numbering systems, plenty of illustrations all go towards improving readability.

Illustrations

Many a good argument is wasted because the writer failed to recognize how it could be reinforced by valid illustrations and tables. These can be invaluable if you are:

- making comparisons between two courses of action or the past versus the present (or future);
- writing for readers who are used to seeing pictorial representations;
- reinforcing subliminal messages, e.g. happy smiling users operating your machinery.

Anticipating and dealing with objections

Someone once described sales proposals as misleading arguments attempting to reach foregone conclusions. Many reports, sales letters and proposals do read that way. It is worthwhile admitting any obvious flaws in your argument at the outset and then setting out how you propose removing or minimizing them. The main fallacies which could trip you up are:

- oversimplification;
- false analogy;
- use of ambiguous words;
- use of misleading illustrations;

- potted thinking;
- sweeping statements;
- reaching false conclusions;
- misleading the reader through conscious omission;
- introducing irrelevant matter into the argument;
- assuming points which have been taken for granted.

Business letters

Dull, clichéd, assumptive and unfriendly—these are just a few of the accusations levelled at business letters. 'Ah, yes,' one client told me, 'but we can't do anything about them as they are on our word processor.' What a fallacious argument. Who composed the word processed letters in the first place? Another word processor? And who says that they cannot be altered, improved or ditched altogether?

First, axe the clichés. Whenever you use a cliché you are using someone else's style, not your own. Most of the following expressions are avoidable—try to substitute a more direct or friendly alternative.

Advise us as to

It is our understanding that

We acknowledge receipt of

Are not in a position to

See our way clear to

May rest assured

In the event of

At which time

It is our understanding

We are of the opinion

In view of the fact that

In the near future

Give consideration to

We are returning herewith

With reference to

In connection with

If you want a model of clarity, succinctness and persuasiveness then study the sales letters sent out in their millions by *Reader's Digest, American Express* and *Time-Life*. Whenever I mention these on my training courses the groans can be heard a mile off. Everyone I know says that they ignore these letters and very often throw them away unopened. This may well be the case. But why do these sales letters make the companies among the richest in the world? Why do their letters generate such a high response? Study them again.

Finally, always finish your letter with a clear statement of what it is that you want your reader to do next. Never leave them in doubt. This is arguably the most important part of your letter—the action line.

Summary

1. Remember the ABC of influential writing: accuracy, briefness, clarity.
2. Use the fog index to sample your own writing style.
3. Think carefully how you would wish your material to be judged. Layout and presentation can go a long way towards making the document appear 'readable'.
4. Think through the physical organization of longer

reports and proposals. Do everything possible to help your readers find their way around your document.

5. Use as many relevant illustrations as possible.
6. Anticipate and deal with objections before they are allowed to arise.
7. Do everything possible to avoid dull, clichéd letters, facsimiles, memos and electronic mail messages.
8. Always finish with a clear statement of what it is you would want your reader to do next.

Appendix: Choosing an influencing model

When it comes to influencing, there is no magic formula. You will not succeed every time. In order to succeed more often and fail less often it is necessary to develop and use a carefully chosen way forward. This way forward will depend on the circumstances and personalities involved. There are several well-known strategies used by influential managers. Try the following three strategies yourself and notice which one(s) suit you and your personal style. Adapt the steps when necessary, making them work for you. Experiment and notice the results. Which approach do you feel most comfortable using? Which one stretches you, makes you develop and grow?

The systematic approach

Use or adapt the following checklist to help plan your approach to influencing in a more systematic fashion:

Step one   Background to my forthcoming influencing situation

(Who will I be influencing? Are they the decision maker or one of a group of decision makers? What will I be influencing them to do or think? When will I carry out my influencing? Will it take one meeting, or many? Where will I conduct the meeting? What will be the advantages/disadvantages of different locations?)

Step two   My specific objectives

(What outcomes do I want? What is the best? Worst? Likely outcome?)

Step three   What do I know about the values and beliefs, needs and wants of the decision maker?
Step four   How will the other person benefit from my proposition?
Step five   What influencing style will work best? Which style will be least productive?
Step six   What are the other person's typical (or probable) decision-making strategies?
Step seven   What is their personality and how might it affect my strategy and tactics?
Step eight   What is my strategy for developing/maintaining good rapport?
Step nine   What objections do I expect? How do I plan to overcome them?
Step ten   How do I plan to obtain a decision?

The soft approach

Stage	Skills necessary
State your view of the problem	♦ Agenda setting ♦ Presentation (do it tentatively) ♦ Seeking feedback
Clarifying others' perceptions	♦ Listening ♦ Reflecting ♦ Questioning ♦ Summarizing

Obtain agreement to
existence of problem

♦ Handling of information
♦ Use of evidence
♦ Handling feedback

Seek solutions
• Propose (see the third model)
• Invite theirs
• Jointly seek compromise/best solution

The harder approach

Stage	Skills necessary
Make proposal	♦ Agenda setting ♦ Assertiveness ♦ Presentation
Obtain reactions	♦ Listening ♦ Questioning ♦ Reflecting
Summarize and check	♦ Summarizing
Deal with objections	♦ Choice of appropriate influencing style or level according to whether commitment or compliance is required ♦ Resistance handling
Outcome	♦ Summarizing ♦ Closing

Source (for the Soft and Harder approaches): Purbrooks

Bibliography

rgyle, Michael, *The Social Psychology of Everyday Life*, London: Routledge, 1992.

ateson, Gregory, *Steps to an Ecology of Mind*, London: Vallentine, 1972.

uzan, Tony, *Use Your Head*, (rev. edn), London: BBC Books, 1989.

uzan, Tony, *The Mind Map Book*, London: BBC Books, 1993.

arnegie, Dale, *How to Win Friends and Influence People*, London: Cedar Books, 1938.

harvet, Shelle Rose, *Words that Change Minds*, Iowa: Kendall/Hunt Publishing, 1995.

opkins, Tom, *How to Master the Art of Selling*, London: Warner Books, 1982.

night, Sue, *NLP at Work*, London: Nicholas Brealey Publishing, 1995.

aborde, Genie, *Influencing with Integrity*, California: Syntony Publishing, 1987.

ambert, Tom, *The Power of Influence*, London: Nicholas Brealey Publishing, 1995.

ease, Allan, *Talk Language*, London: Simon & Schuster, 1989.

Rackham, Neil, *Spin®-Selling*, Aldershot: Gower Publishing Limited, 1995.

Richardson, Jerry, *The Magic of Rapport*, California: Meta Publications, 1987.

Index